The Tragedy of the Ocean Monarch

Colin Reed

Published by Colin Reed, 2021.

THE TRAGEDY OF THE OCEAN MONARCH

First edition. September 23, 2021.

ISBN: 979-8231460076

Written by Colin Reed.

Table of Contents

FORWARD....1
THE SHIP AND LAUNCHING....13
THE DOCKSIDE AT LIVERPOOL....21
CHARTISTS....31
THE DISCOVERY OF THE FIRE AS THE TRAGEDY UNFOLDS....43
THE RESCUERS, THE BURNING SHIP, THE SURVIVORS' STORIES AND THE DEAD....65
THE LAST ONES OFF....95
THE END OF THE RESCUE....105
THE BODIES....109
THE INQUESTS....131
THE DEE PILOT, QUEEN OF CHESTER....135
THE NEW WORLD ACCOUNT....139
THE LIVING AND THE RETURN TO THE SHORE..147
THE PARLIAMENTRAY VERDICT....177
THE RECOVERY OF THE WRECK....181
THE DOM AFONSO (POSTSCRIPT)....189
MIGRANT SHIP SAFETY....191
FREDERICK JEROME....207
JOTHAM BRAGDON....215
ALICE WRIGLEY....219
PASSENGER LISTS....225
SOURCES AND ACKNOWLEDGEMENTS....233
THE OLD SEAFARER AND THE AUTHOR....237

Table of Contents

Thanks to Alex Reed for the design of the cover image and to My wife Barbara Reed for her continuing support

FORWARD

In the churchyard of the parish church of All Hallows, Bispham, a district of the larger township of Blackpool on the northwest coast of England, UK, is a gravestone belonging to Alice Wrigley. Alice's gravestone, now lying flat, reads, with a dedication from her sister above it; ... 'She perished at Sea in the endeavour to escape from the Wreck of the Ship OCEAN MONARCH when on Fire 26 August 1848'.

As a technical detail, it was actually Thursday the 24th August when the Ocean Monarch, in its tragic demise, was subject to a fierce and uncontrollable conflagration, and eventually sunk off the North Wales coast just a few hours into its journey from Liverpool en route to Boston in America. But in the enormity of the tragedy, a technical detail can't be given too much importance in the instruction of the bereaved to the monumental mason.

In its regular function as a packet ship carrying news from Europe and a cargo of goods, the Ocean Monarch was carrying about three hundred and fifty passengers, the vast majority of these being emigrants, all with dreams of a new life on the other side of the Atlantic. Alice was one of about one hundred and seventy passengers who lost their lives in the tragedy, their bodies ignominiously washed up on the northwest coasts of Wales and England, or dragged out of the sea by a passing vessel in the days and weeks after the tragedy, and one unidentified body recovered from the wreck during salvage operations deep under water sometime later.

In the absence of TV cameras or the personal video facility of the mobile phone, the incident has nevertheless been recorded in sketches and paintings, sometimes perhaps with the opportunity for a little acceptable imagination in their transcriptions, where the camera, traditionally doesn't lie, at least away from the influences of modern technology. All these representations of the event have been created from the original, conceived as an eye witness during the event by the Prince de Joinville from the Brazilian frigate the Dom Afonso which was on a trial run after its recent construction and launching in Liverpool and, fortunately for many who survived, coming across the tragedy by chance and able to save the lives of those many. A representation of this sketch and the relative positions of some of the boats involved in the rescue at the time was printed in the Illustrated London News 2nd September 1848. The steam packet ship, the Prince of Wales, originally on its way to Bangor, is seen in the background and the lug sail of the yacht, the Queen of the Ocean on its way back from Beaumaris is seen in between the ships. The other major player in the rescue, the packet ship New World, leaving Liverpool at the same time as the Ocean Monarch is not seen, but this sketched view of the tragedy would have been evident from the decks of that ship and not the Dom Afonso. Understandably perhaps the Prince de Joinville, in an example of product placement, might have wanted to see his national Brazilian flag featured. The small boats from all these vessels are in the water struggling with the sea conditions in brave and exhausting efforts, which resulted in the rescuing of over half of the four hundred or so passengers and crew on board.

Of the many who lost their lives on that day during the tragic and dramatic shipwreck there are several unidentified bodies buried in the same Bispham churchyard, lifeless bodies now, but long since free of the fear and pain of burning or drowning and the frightening and helpless separation from close family members, and which had been cast upon the beach and the responsibility of the administrative parish of the time, to bury. Alice's is one of those several bodies, most discovered in a badly decomposed state, whose last resting place was on this Fylde Coast rather than their dream of reaching America.

To date, from recorded times, the coast with its strong, south westerly winds and its insidiously hidden sandbanks situated near both the beginning and the end of a transatlantic shipping route, has seen the wrecks of over a hundred and fifty ships and it is also the grave of many a seafarer, as much of the coastlines of Britain have been, and all which have their stories to tell. The Norfolk coastline was the last resting place of another Alice, a Bamber, from Blackpool, shipwrecked and buried at Caistor ten years after the tragedy of the Ocean Monarch and, as the wife of the captain, and sailing with him and their young son, she would have been fully well aware of that recent tragedy, though she probably had blocked from her mind the fact that it could actually happen to her as she might have passed the other Alice's headstone during a contemplative sojourn in the churchyard below the former whitewashed tower of its church.

Whilst, on the other hand, the shore dwellers of any coastline can take advantage of the bounty of the sea in providing unexpected bonuses of wrecked cargo, the first instinctive and intrinsically human duty of those possessing a higher moral code and which belongs to most shore dwellers, is always to regard the welfare of those that can be rescued, and to give the respect to those who couldn't be, by providing them with a respectable burial. Anything up for grabs as the free pickings of booty before the customs men arrived, was secondary to the compassionate and fair-minded human being, and this applies to any coastline.

Not only were bodies from the Ocean Monarch deposited on these northwest shores after the incident but, with the wind changing to a south westerly, each of the two daily tides on the Fylde Coast delivered charred debris from the wreck along with the figurehead of the ship, the damaged head of Neptune, the maritime deity with whom both the ship and nearly half of its human cargo were now residing.

There had always been the occasional body washed upon these shores and, at this date, an expected legal recompense for finding one and reporting it to the authorities, though on this occasion there were sadly more than usual. Nearly ten years later, in 1857 it is reported that a man called Robert Bamber came across a body floating in the sea at the water's edge. He went immediately to report the incident to the police since he was aware that there was a 5s (25p and just short of £24) reward for finding a body in this way. Had he thought more, he could have brought the body out of the water and saved the life of a man who was not actually dead but more likely to have suffered a fit at the water's edge as the later inquest concluded. But there would be no 5s reward if the body was found on the shore, which makes sense in a particular way as it would naturally result in many bodies being dumped on the beach under the cover of darkness and a queue a mile long outside the newly constructed police station waiting for a reward. Such is always potentially shown the darker side of the human individual in its lower moral code in which selfish opportunism can rise far above conscience. Of course, in Robert Bamber's defence, he might not have known that the body was still alive. That natural human condition of selfishness however, was far less evident in the events played out during the burning of the Ocean Monarch when, in defiance of death, life was risked in order to save the lives of strangers, occasionally polar opposites in socio-economics, politics and religion.

An unlikely and distant influence in the recounting of this story belongs to a certain Johann Cofty, related to the writer of this and a survivor of a shipwreck from the HMS Sceptre nearly fifty years earlier in Capetown. In his desperation and determination to survive he clung onto a timber in the heavy, rolling seas, like many would do later from the Ocean Monarch. For him, eventually reaching the shore, he later took a stroll along the shoreline when he was out of hospital and bemoaned the fact that the bodies of many of his former naval shipmates, some with whom he was at loggerheads, were sticking out of their shallow graves on the beach and being eaten by the pigs. Along the northwest coasts of England and Wales those bodies on the Ocean Monarch were able to receive the respectfully more permanent burials that time and opportunity allowed.

Since the bodies from the Ocean Monarch had been in the sea for quite some time, they were mostly disfigured, and identification was largely through wearing apparel and personal effects, but in some cases even this was not possible. In Alice's case, her clothes were recognised by her sister as they were hanging on the church hedge in the hope that, as well as the practical idea of drying, more importantly, they might provide identification to any of the bodies. Her family had bid her farewell at the docks at Liverpool but, before they had returned home to Bury, their home town, the news of the tragedy broke. With no news of her among the survivors landed from the rescue boats, her distraught father had scoured the seaside places of Wales, the Wirral peninsula and further north to search for any news of her. When it was discovered that one of the bodies washed up on the Fylde coast might be that of his daughter, he was not able to confront the reality of the truth himself. While he might have eventually got to sleep during those long days and nights always in the agonies of waiting for news, accompanied by a determined hope, and waking up with the same defiant grip on hope that she might yet be alive perhaps, when he was eventually presented with the reality, he was too upset to undertake the identification in person, and he left it to his other daughter, Alice's sister. Alice's mother, is not mentioned in the reports of her demise but it is more than likely that she was a member of the family farewell party and was as equally distraught as her husband. It was an age when a man, as pater familias, was given a mention and a woman, just as important as mater familias, represented in many a single mother today, couldn't be considered as much, and wasn't. Alice's sister, herself needing not only directions to the outlying village of Bispham from her accommodation in Blackpool, but also probably some moral support, was accompanied by a sympathetic person from that lodging house in which she had stayed overnight.

More bodies were washed up further north at Fleetwood, Cockerham Sands, Glasson Dock, Heysham, Hest Bank, Silverdale and as far as the Kent estuary near Milnthorpe, and to the south, on the Wirral peninsula, the Welsh coast, or picked out of the sea in between, about a hundred and seventy in all.

The demise of the Ocean Monarch is every bit as spectacular and tragic as the more recent and persistent loss of the Titanic and which has more precedence over other shipwrecks in the popular mindset. The heavy loss of passengers on the Ocean Monarch included those who were either burnt to death or drowned, or perhaps more mercifully killed instantly under the crushing impact of falling timbers or in a single, reported instance as the one woman who cut her throat as the better alternative to drowning as she wavered between life and death, the fire raging above and behind her and the sea beckoning below her, are as dramatic and fearful as those involved with the Titanic and there are some parallels with the two events, too. The ship burnt for nearly three hours, from about noon to 3pm, before the last two desperate survivors still on the ship and too afraid to jump, were finally rescued by an act of supreme bravery from a single human individual among a team of tireless and professionally skilled men, manning the rowing boats from those ships within reach, with equally tireless strength in difficult sea conditions.

Artefacts brought up from the Titanic and the more complete knowledge and understanding from the records of that ship, give an attachment to it that the lack of memory and the distance in time, which break the connectivity of the names of those involved in the Ocean Monarch, no longer have. The horror of the event and the compassion elicited from it for those adversely affected by it has been watered down by the passage of time, the echoes of their screams for mercy and the pleas for the preservation of each unique life no longer audible.

The story of the loss of the ocean Monarch is also, quite vividly, a time capsule of the age which becomes evident when the story is revealed. 1848 was a troubled year in Europe, when there were riots or insurrections and unrest leading to fighting in the streets throughout Europe. Hungary, France, Germany, Italy, Sicily, Spain, Austria, Prussia, Ireland and the demands of Chartism in England were all represented in the disruption and violence and often the reason why packet ships like the Ocean Monarch were full of a contingent of emigrants fleeing from the trouble and hoping for a free and fulfilled life of their own making elsewhere.

There had always been the human characteristics of liberalism and conservatism in national politics but these now had to contend with the rising need of the developing 'left wing' of a social movement which would now include the bulk of the population, the manufacturing working classes that needed and demanded a voice and the right for the equality of opportunity to take what they needed from society as much as they had given to it. Kingdoms whose subjects were allowed their limited freedoms at the monarch's pleasure, had been called into question, and these 'subjects' now wanted a say in the conduct of their lives and their destinies. Liberty as a concept was in the collective consciousness and, as Macaulay wrote in the following year, liberty had to be sacrificed in order to save civilisation, or in the words of Benjamin Franklin, 'those who would give up essential liberty to purchase a little temporary safety, deserve neither liberty nor safety.' Both concepts which are represented in most human conflict to justify either side of it, are only able to be resolved, where compromise cannot be included, through conflict. Conditions had reached an ignition point. Just as a spark had dropped onto the combustible material in the Ocean

Monarch to cause a severe conflagration, Europe was burning furiously after the ignition from its own spark of social unrest.

The Sun newspaper, as a broadsheet, and not the later tabloid, reported on 30th December 1848, 'Month after month the noise of the "agonies of great nations" has resounded to us across the waters of the Channel – the detonations of those social earthquakes which have subverted thrones, shaken cities into ruin, driven forth the most powerful statesmen as fugitives, and strewn the earth with the cadaverous relics of civil battle.' Some of those displaced statesmen would find themselves as witnesses to the tragedy of the Ocean Monarch, even giving assistance to members of a demographic group identified as those who, ironically, might have caused their displacement and exile in the first place. Liberty has a wide meaning and interpretation, and history would show that the natural selfishness of the collective human individual would assure that society would move in cycles rather than being able to reach and maintain a utopian level of existence with fairness for all and where all can be happy 'in saecula saeculorum'. Liberty might be gained through pain and sorrow and, once gained, lost with complacency when the naturally intrinsic self-interest of the human individual is let loose when the opportunity presents itself.

The Ocean Monarch had left Liverpool, a town with its large Irish population, and was bound for Boston, equally with its large Irish population and the ship itself had a large Irish contingent, but it only reached as far as the coast of North Wales. In the tragic events that materialised on the late Thursday morning and early afternoon of August 24th of that year, the intrinsic compassion of the human being came to the fore thus demonstrating that the human being in all its tragedies, conflicts and uncertainties could show the higher moral side to its character in acts of supreme bravery and self-sacrifice exercised by those who saw a fellow human being in need and thus overriding the suspicions and prejudices of race, politics, class or religion which forever permeate mixed society.

Much of the story is about emigration. From England in the previous year of 1847, 258,270 people emigrated, which was a number claimed to be twice as great as any other year. Some of these included Irish railway navvies working on the proliferation of the railways and who had saved up enough cash to move to the wide open spaces of America. And there were emigrants from all trades and labours, not only from Britain and Ireland but from all over Europe making their way from several Continental ports.

It was estimated, or claimed, at the time that the social conditions of the United Kingdom created about a hundred and fifty thousand folk who lived by 'theft and idleness in want'. There was plenty of space for them in the wide open spaces of the unsettled territories and crown lands, 200,000,000 acres (nearly 81 million hectares) in all in North America. It was also convenient to fund emigration for those who could not afford the passage money, nor had the funds to set themselves up once they had arrived. In areas of large unemployment it was easier and more economical to get rid of those who had become dependent upon the poor rate through the economic downturn of industry. Emigration was seen as the cure for many a socio-economic need. The Government funded Emigration Committee, would describe as its slogan for anybody able to undertake the voyage, 'Let the English operative weigh these things, and inquire whether emigration be not the truest kindness to himself as well as to both the countries in question.' Perhaps, in a cynical interpretation it could mean, 'go away, you're no good to us anymore. Try your luck somewhere else and those who remain can reap the profit of your departure.'

An incentive created in the Potteries in North Staffordshire by the employers comprised of a contribution fund, possibly an appeasement to the potential of destructive strikes within the working classes which had 'blighted the pottery industry for the last eighteen years.' Consequently the pottery owners had bought up sixteen hundred acres of land in Wisconsin, America where twenty acres could be bought for a single one at home in the UK. Not surprisingly, and without stretching imaginations for those who wanted to give it a name, it was called Pottersville. Here in this privately funded and contributory, 'Potter's Emigration Plan', the worker could contribute a weekly amount of 6d (2½p; £2.03p) for each share of £1(£81.01p) 1s 6d (£1 7½p; £6.08p) and from which there would be a qualification for a ballot to the right of emigration. It seems that it worked like a kind of lottery, the winner receiving the funding to emigrate via loan and grant. This would ensure supporting funds for a twenty acre (a very little over 8 hectares) farm at a cost of £5.10s (£5.50p; £445.56p) for which the society's funds would forward most of the cost, (£4 8s 6d; £4 42½p; £358.47p). The fund would cover the cost of breaking up the land, sowing cereal crops, fencing the land and building the log cabin, and credit would be given for twelve months' supply of provisions and the money advanced being repayable within ten years. The success of this enterprise in its early stages, and according to its supporters, was demonstrated by the fact that of fifty families already out there, who at home had been staring the workhouse in the face, were now enjoying the best of health and not one of them would consider returning home. This promotional brag of course was not the whole truth as the scheme failed in 1849 and not everyone was successful, some returning home. The specific skills of a potter, quite understandably, could not necessarily turn a hand to the rigours and skills of farming and house building at the same time so easily and so necessarily quickly in the urgency of the circumstances. As far as the potters might have been concerned it could be considered ironic that the Ocean Monarch was carrying several tons of china for customers in Boston.

In November of 1848, not long after the tragedy of the Ocean Monarch when the risk of sea travel was still worth it, the six hundred ton Britannia left the London docks bound for Australia with emigrants from several nations, French, German and Irish and there was a whole fleet of vessels waiting by the jetty to take on more emigrants for the same destination. In Australia work was readily available and a labourer could earn £20 (£2, 434.53p) a year with accommodation sometimes thrown in, and living described as very cheap.

More than fifteen hundred journeymen Swiss watch and clockmakers from Neufchatel had emigrated heading for America to leave behind them the distress of the Continent-wide revolutions and sought a more peaceful life elsewhere. More folk who wanted to be liberated from the inadequate or failed societies were making preparations from all parts of Europe, to follow too.

But, among the passengers and its rescuers of the Ocean Monarch, there is also the story of an escaping bank robber, a secretly eloping couple who'd left their families behind them, a suspected murderer, a Brazilian revolutionary, a displaced French monarch, class conflict in England, the insensitivity of Irish Land Laws and the safety, or lack of safety, of sea travel. Few passenger ships of the day carried sufficient lifeboats and the Titanic over sixty years later reprised that deficiency though the fire that raged below decks on that ship had been kept under control for the entire journey until its premature ending. The Ocean Monarch had four life boats, not enough to accommodate even a quarter of the ship's contingent of passengers and crew. Two of these were successfully used for escape by just a few people who managed to get into them, and two were burnt to cinders before they could be used as there was no crew left to man them.

The steerage passengers, those that could be stuffed below decks in large numbers, were the bread and butter of these voyages, their money financed the ships' companies and made them profitable more so than the cargo that the ships carried. Their berths were the cheapest, but there were more of them, and large numbers could be packed in. Most of them were poor and easily considered by the more privileged elements of society as unimportant and even dispensable, a disparity which caused the conflict from which most of them were fleeing anyway.

Some of those who stayed behind in their homelands by choice or inability to travel would find themselves in either civil or international conflict. And some did so either in the streets or waving the collective flag of their nations as the war in the Crimea was not very far away. Some of those who fled to America, anyway, might have found themselves fighting as the conditions for a vicious and bloody civil conflict were developing towards a flashpoint in that land.

But, of course, all the countries of the new worlds already had their indigenous populations who had no place in the dreams and the ambitions of these masses of immigrants. Such is the potential admix of circumstance and opportunism in the naturally selfish sense of survival of the human individual.

THE SHIP AND LAUNCHING

The new and impressive packet ship, the Ocean Monarch, which turned heads in admiration at its entry into port at each consistent end of its regular transatlantic journey had, sadly, only a short lived existence, its record breaking crossings of the Atlantic from Boston to Liverpool and back, were ended in dramatic fashion on that fateful day at the end of August 1848. The result of an allegedly careless spark dropped onto a highly combustible, wooden sailing vessel was witnessed off the North Wales coast, and by those drawn to its rescue in which, for some, to risk a life to save a life was considered a responsibility as part of the higher moral code within the human condition. The ship was only hours into the voyage with its cargo of goods and passengers, mostly emigrants with anxious hopes of reaching a different life in the New World. The vessel having caught fire, burnt to the water's edge and sunk, but not before about a hundred and seventy passengers either succumbed to the inferno itself, or drowned in escaping from the fire and the molten metals and pitch, into the cold and dangerous roughness of the sea. Many of the steerage passengers in their berths below decks were slumbering away the sea sickness of an unaccustomed mode of travel, and there would be a large number among them from the inland towns who would have never even seen the sea before the day they had arrived into the hustle and bustle of Liverpool's busy and noisy docks.

The Ocean Monarch was a packet ship, a ship that made regular voyages from port to port with news, cargo and passengers either on a commission or a charter basis. It was built by Donald McKay at the shipyards in East Boston and launched at high water at twenty three minutes past ten o'clock on the morning of Saturday 12th June 1847. At over three hundred tons it was a hundred and seventy seven feet long, had what was described as a generous depth of hold, and three decks. At the time it was one of the largest merchantmen ever built in the USA, and most certainly the largest in Boston. It was built for Enoch Train of the Train & Co line of Liverpool to Boston packets, and it was commanded by Captain Murdoch. Converted into metric measurements, the vessel was generally over sixty two metres long and over twelve metres wide. The main mast was over twenty seven metres tall and the yard nearly twenty three metres square. Of a fine design and finish, the timbers used were of a good quality and section, and the furnishings and decoration in the cabins were of a high class.

A month later, the Boston News of the 7th July 1847, could eulogise about the pride and joy of Boston's shipbuilding skills with a detailed analysis of the structure of the vessel. In its description, unless obscurely technical shipbuilding terms roll off the tongue in quantity like those of a favourite subject spoken with enthusiasm round a pub table with friends of shared interests, then without an instructive diagram in front of you, it would make difficult reading. For those knowledgeable of the structure of wooden sailing ships however, it is described, and optional whether a ship is considered he, she or it, verbatim as thus; 'The new and beautiful vessel sails today on her first voyage to Liverpool. She is the largest merchant ship belonging to this port, and is very heavily timbered and strongly fastened. Her keel is 168 feet long in two depths which, combined, 32 inches deep by 18 inches wide. Her stem is 16 feet by 12 at the bottom, and 16 by 18 at the top; floor timbers 18 inches moulded in the thrust and sided 12. She has three depths of midship keelsons, in all 4 feet 2 inches deep by 16 inches wide; sister keelsons 14 by 15 inches, and bilge keelsons 12 by 15 and her scantling stout in proportion, bolted, and otherwise fastened in the same style as the packet ship New World of New York. The Ocean Monarch is 179 feet 9 inches long on deck, a 190 feet from the knight heads to the taffel and, having a head which projects 14 feet, makes her length between her extremes 204 feet. She has 40 feet breadth of beam, 27 feet depth of hold, and is about 1,301 tons and a fraction, custom house measurement. The whole rake of her stern is 10 feet, and her stern post 12 inches. She has 20 inches dead rise at half floor, 16 inches swell of sides, and 2 feet 2 inches sheer. Her scantling is principally of yellow pine, but her frame, knees, breast hooks, and stanchions are the best seasoned white oak and hacmatac. She has three decks, and a topgallant forecastle – the last the height of the main rail, and extends aft to the windlass. The upper deck is not a mere hurricane deck, supported on the ends of the bulwark stanchions etc but is as complete as the upper deck of any other ship. The height from the lower to the middle deck is 7 feet, and between the decks above it, is 7 feet 6 inches, which leaves her 12 foot 6 inches depth of hold below the lower deck. The lower deck is entirely clear fore and aft; on the middle deck she has three cabins, which extend to the mainmast, and a forecastle for the crew forward. Her main cabin or dining saloon is aft, and is finished with mahogany, enamelled pilasters, gilt work & in the most magnificent style, and is furnished with almost oriental splendour. The ladies' cabin, which is before it, is ditto, ditto and a little more. The second class passengers' cabin contains all that is necessary to ensure comfort and convenience. Her state-rooms are large and, like her cabins, amply and elegantly furnished, well lighted and ventilated. Both decks have patent side-lights, and are otherwise well adapted for the comfort of steerage passengers; and every passage from the upper deck which leads below is protected from the rain or salt water. She has a wheel-house, in the starboard side of which is the entrance to the main cabin; and abaft the main-mast a house covers the passage to the second cabin. A large house between the fore and the main hatchways contains apartments for galleys, stock, ice, coals etc etc and also covers two stairways which lead to the deck below. Under the topgallant forecastle are several water-closets, lockers etc. She is very roomy on deck and looks magnificently. All her decks are white pine, the planks 3½ inches thick by 6 inches wide and are remarkably clear of flaws and knots. Her bulwarks are surmounted with a monkey rail, and the inside of her main rail is lined with copper fore and aft.'

'Her head terminates in a full figure of Neptune, but her bow requires no such ornament to set it off. Indeed her model has been pronounced by all who have seen her as the most symmetrical in its proportions of any vessel, large or small that has yet been built in this vicinity. Her ends are very sharp, but still her lines are rounded with such perfect exactness that as a whole she seems as complete as a circle. Her stern is slight and curves most beautifully from the transom upwards and from the quarter timbers across. Neptune and his rib seated on a car drawn by nondescripts and relieved by scrollwork, form an arch over her cabin window. The ground of the stern is black, her name and port of hail white, her head is all white and her hull black with painted ports in a white streak. Her sheer is graduated to a hair, and her planking outside is as smooth as glass and very regular in size, that on the wales being 7 inches thick by 6 wide and on the waist 5 inches square. In finish throughout she is more like a pleasure yacht than a large merchant ship. Her mainmast is 89 feet long, her main yard 75 feet square, and her other spars in proportion. Her masts and yards are as well designed as her hull, and seem all that the eye could desire to render her a perfect ship. She has pole topgallant and royal masts, and is not disfigured with gunter masts courting acquaintance with the clouds. Her yards and bowsprit are black, and her lower masts etc white. There is nothing which calls for special notice in the style of rig, but of course, her rigging and spars are of the best materials to correspond with the hull. When launched she drew 112 feet of water, and floated on an even keel; her sailing trim, therefore when loaded will be in proportion. That she will sail fast and work well, no one at all acquainted with a ship can doubt; indeed, it will be difficult for any vessel to outsail her when in proper trim. She was built and sparred by Mr Donald McKay, is owned by Messrs Enoch Train and Co., and is commanded by Capt. Murdoch, who is one of the most successful ship-masters belonging to Boston. Col Enoch Train who originated the line of packets to which the Ocean Monarch has just been added, is entitled to praise for the energy, in the face of many discouragements, he has displayed, in rendering his line as perfect as it can be. Better ships no nation can boast, than those which have been built under his auspices. (The Ocean Monarch has lately arrived in Liverpool).'

As a detail, and not recorded in the eulogy of its design, the tin and planished ware was provided by Andrew Peterson of Washington Street in Boston.

A large crowd had gathered on the dockside in celebratory mood to equal that of a 4th July occasion to witness the launch of the Ocean Monarch into 'Neptune's bosom' or, 'the deep and restless blue'. Yachts and pleasure boats and the steamer Mayflower were all bedecked with flags as was the Ocean Monarch itself. The American jack, flew from the bowsprit, a flag which would, in just over a year's time signal its distress by being displayed upside down, as was the tradition to indicate distress, and in this tragic case it would be a prelude to the ship's complete demise. The British ensign flew from the foremast, the owner's private signal flag (red with a white centred diamond) from the main mast, identifying signal numbers from the mizzen mast, and 'the glorious stripes and stars flaunted gaily over the stern.' Over 1300 tons of this glorious vessel slid down the slipway to the waves and the cheers of the assembled crowd and 'nothing could be more imposingly beautiful afloat as it entered the water'. Instead of champagne, a bottle of anchor brand temperance bitter, manufactured especially for this occasion was smashed against its head by chief mate Mr Patten. Proud to be from Boston, the cheers of the crowd reached a crescendo when the ship majestically entered the water, after which it was towed by the steamer Mayflower to the Lewis wharf where Enoch Train had his warehouses.

There is a little anecdote in one of the papers which recounts the story of poor old, tearful Mrs Partington who had eagerly attended the launching and who, after waiting for over an hour, bent down momentarily to tie her shoe lace at the crucial time and missed the whole affair. But it wasn't that the launch was lightning fast, or that her shoes had been provided with exceptionally long shoe laces or, perhaps, that there was some other complexity or physical difficulty in tying them up. In the end it was the reporter having a joke at the expense of the generic old, fictitious woman that Mrs Partington was, and to whom misfortune came very easily and regularly. Well known on both sides of the Atlantic, the readership would be well acquainted with her and perhaps smile in their reading as she was subject to the cruel wit of his comedic fun. It was a misfortune however, which could have happened to anyone, though not recorded in factual truth that it did.

The celebration of the launch was an exciting time with no sense of foreboding of the tragedy that was to come in a little more than a year's time. But, after the launching when fictional Mrs Partington, or her unfortunate, real life counterparts would be wending their disappointed ways home, a sumptuous meal was given for the mariners and the ship workers at the moulding rooms of Mr McKay, followed by the children of the district. There were speeches made and sentiments expressed, but the only recorded words are that of an 'old tar', who is probably Captain Murdoch since he is formerly of the Joshua Bates about which he eulogises in impromptu manner while stood upon a tar barrel, perhaps with his bottle held aloft in the hand of his extended arm, 'The Joshua Bates was the tallest beauty ever built; but this craft is a head and shoulders taller than her – she can't be capped, so it's no use to try.' No doubt true, but the honesty of his impromptu enthusiasm smacks of a glass of rum or two, rather than temperance beer unless, in the extent of his enthusiasm, he hadn't needed the supportive assistance of alcohol. Captain James Murdoch was a veteran of the Liverpool run across the Atlantic in the Joshua Bates albeit a ship of six hundred tons only, being less than half the size of his new ship, the Ocean Monarch.

While the ship had still been under construction in May, the design of the ship to follow it in construction in the shipyard was already on the table, and immediately after the launch of the Ocean Monarch in June, the keel of this other ship, the Anglo American, was put down. At the same time there was a merry go round of captaincies as James Murdoch moved from the Joshua Bates, named after the financier and his father of the same name and a director of Baring Brothers, the Liverpool agents for the shipping line of the Ocean Monarch, to the Ocean Monarch, and Captain Albert Brown would move from the Mary Ann to the new ship under construction, the Anglo American. The first mate, Mr Patten of the Ocean Monarch, then will move as captain to the Mary Ann.

By the 26th June the ship was rigged ready for sailing and the loading could begin, the date set for the first voyage being July 7th at high tide. With a full load of freight, there were also twenty seven cabin passengers on board and twenty travelling steerage. To those many who saw beauty in a sailing ship in both the symmetry and completion of the design and also its function, they could comfortably watch as, 'She floats on an even keel and draws twenty one feet of water but, notwithstanding this great displacement, she appears flying light, her upper deck being nearly twelve feet above the load line.' A regular sailing day would be the 5th of the month which would work out as every two months for a round trip including loading and unloading. A first cabin would cost $80 ($2,637) and a second cabin $50 ($1650) but no price at the time given for a steerage passage ticket. Perhaps this was considered beneath the dignity of the moment in the proud promotion of such a vessel. However, prices quoted elsewhere are $10 ($329) as the lowest price or, from Liverpool in sterling, it was actually £5 (£405.06p) for the upper steerage deck and less for the lower steerage deck). The ship was reported to have arrived at Liverpool on the last day of July, though the journey would eventually take a regular sixteen days or so.

And so, on its penultimate journey, the Boston Post of 9th March 1848 can record with repeated pride of a ship built in its own shipyard, 'The splendid packet ship Ocean Monarch, Capt Murdoch, will sail tomorrow, weather permitting, on her third voyage to Liverpool. Capt. Murdoch, to his credit be it stated, has kept his beautiful ship in most excellent order. Nothing seems wanting in her, below or aloft, to render her one of the most perfect ships that ever floated.'

But, ultimately, all this beauty, technical brilliance and achievement, stood no chance against the gross error of human carelessness, a dropped match or a carelessly unprotected candle in the darkness of the lower decks, either by a steerage passenger or a steward, both of who were regarded as a lower social status and intelligence and were convenient to blame.

THE DOCKSIDE AT LIVERPOOL

The potential horrors of a long journey by sea did not deter the travellers from throwing in their lot with fortune, whether they'd been warned or teased about these ships eventually being referred to as coffin ships or not. Such were the hardships or dissatisfactions that many of the emigrants endured in their homelands that many thousands had thought it was worth the risk, if not entirely urged on by the focus of potential prosperity. Though there were always those who died naturally anyway en route due to the rigours of the journey, fire was always a greater risk on a wooden ship and, as demonstrated so tragically by the Ocean Monarch, it could take many healthy lives all in one go. Some sixty four years or so later the fire in the Titanic lasted from its launch in Belfast almost to the moment of the collision with the iceberg. Stokers working twenty four hours a day in shifts contained the fire by methodically moving the burning coals from their storage into the furnaces. To the despair of those attempting to contain the fire, the excess had been put out by the time the ship hit the iceberg. They had been helped in their task by the iron compartmentalisation of the ship's structure. If it had been a wooden ship then presumably, like the Ocean Monarch before it, it would have been an inferno in the few hours after leaving port. Ship design had evolved by 1912 but the consideration of passengers hadn't, and lessons evidently hadn't been learnt or at least, taken seriously.

So for the determined émigré, with a ticket as little as £5 (£405.06p) and cheaper still to Canada, a British colony, there were millions of unsettled acres that were able to support more than the population of Britain. There was work for all from unskilled labourers to the professions. Labourers could expect 6s.5d (32½p approx.: £14.17p) a day and some skilled workers 7s 6d (37½p; £30.38) a day. There was space and beauty in the landscape to banish the penury and claustrophobia of the workforce in Britain. For those with a little bit of money there were favourable terms on the loan of capital for land or buildings. There was so much incentive in the New World for a fresh start and to accomplish dreams unattainable at home, and anybody with a bit of nerve, the minimum of cash, or in some cases, the desperate need to run away from something, could take the opportunity.

The three decker Ocean Monarch, the 'splendid packet ship' of thirteen hudred tons, (1320.861 tonnes) having been launched for the Train's lines of Liverpool packets on Saturday 12th June 1847 at East Boston with James Murdoch as captain, was just one of more than twenty thousand ships providing over three million tons of goods to the port of Liverpool and over £3m (£359,778,947.37), in revenue for the port, annually.

Many of the ships would be regular visitors to the port and when the 'beautiful new ship', Ocean Monarch arrived at Liverpool for the first time it would no doubt have created a great impression and also without doubt, there would have been a keenness among many interested parties to take a diversion to view it as it sat at the dockside. It would have been the excitable talk of the dockside with the language of the merchants in the Exchange Rooms excited about its looks and its profit-making potential being different to the language of the dock workers and the mariners in the alehouses, all professionally competent and excited about its speed, its function and its structure. Each of these polar opposites in social status would nevertheless share the same ability to appreciate and reach their own conclusions, whatever the chosen expletive to express these conclusions might be. It was important to state that the ship carried a surgeon, a further compliment to its greater status.

Its regular cargo consisted of cotton bales, flour, Indian corn, cheese, bacon, and turpentine. At a merchandise broker's sale after its November arrival in Liverpool in 1847, twenty barrels of American lard were up for auction. In December of 1847 there were still a hundred and twelve barrels and thirteen tierces (smaller barrels) of American lard from the recent cargo of the Ocean Monarch to be auctioned off from the Exchange Buildings. Prior to that on the 14th of August 1847, the Hull advertiser announced the arrival of a 'vessel named the Ocean Monarch' in which the cargo consisted of 3,734 barrels of flour, 42 barrels of soda biscuits, 200 boxes of soda crackers, 400 barrels and bags of bread, 283 barrels of beans, 227 barrels of corn-meal, 274 barrels of corn bran, 321 barrels of an article called 'wheat shorts', 4,833 sacks of corn, 200 boxes of cheese, and extensive cargo.' The problem with this is that the report is of a ship landing its cargo in the Thames, but its description of 1300 tons burden from Boston would surely refer to the Ocean Monarch of the Trains Lines and there is no specific date or even evidence for its arrival in London.

Once at port, the unloading could begin and the cargo was taken to the extensive warehouses on the docks and sold or auctioned off there. Some of this cargo would have gone to the warehouses of Thomas Littledale, a merchant of Liverpool and who on that Thursday morning in August was enjoying a casual return on his yacht from a sailing regatta at Beaumaris and who, along with friends and crew aboard, was one of the first to be drawn into the tragedy of the burning ship and its screaming, burning, pleading passengers. The cargo of the Ocean Monarch for its journey back across the Atlantic Ocean to Boston consisted, in the testimony of the mate, Jotham Bragdon, at the subsequent inquest, of iron, salt, hardware and earthenware, along with provisions for eighty days out at sea and 'principally of beef, pork, flour, rice and other things.' Butter was stored in kegs in the stewards' room and bread and flour was stored in the rear store room.

Enoch Train, the owner of Train's Lines, was a well-respected man in the world of ocean commerce, and other ships belonging to the Line, included the Milton, Mary Anne, Anglo American and Washington Irving. They were all advertised as first class ships, as copper bottomed and copper fastened, (it has also been reported that joint British ownership of a vessel would have ensured the attachment of a copper bottom before a return across the Atlantic after its first voyage if one hadn't been provided), sailed by men of good experience and with excellent accommodation for passengers, proud boasts which belied the fact that they only carried enough boats for just a few people in case of emergency and that perhaps those passengers who could only afford to travel steerage and who had to bring along their own straw to sleep on might not have wanted to agree with the claims of excellent accommodation. The American built ships however, like the Ocean Monarch, had to conform to stricter US Passenger Laws which required more space and a more generous food allocation for steerage passengers than a ship registered in Britain.

The Ocean Monarch was the largest of the fleet and the pride of the Line. A ship sailed from Boston on the 5th of every month, and goods arrangements had to be concluded by the 18th of the previous month. The journey to Boston was the shortest route to America from Liverpool. If you wanted a shorter journey you would go via Southampton but the Trains Lines were simply the Liverpool/Boston route. It took about sixteen and a half days (though the journey out of Liverpool on 17th September 1847 took twenty three and a half days for some reason) of cramped conditions for steerage, and the rolling of the ship to the unaccustomed passengers invited much sea sickness, and many on the ill-fated journey the following year were lying and groaning in their discomfort upon their beds as the fire took hold in the few hours only of sailing from Liverpool.

It wasn't always plain sailing for the magnificent vessel though, for on May 22nd 1848, the Ocean Monarch arrived in Boston bringing three hundred passengers, most presumably emigrants and there was reason to state that they were all in good health, implying that even the strongest and healthiest of passengers were usually pretty much shook up and pale by the end of what would have been an arduous journey for all. It also had valuable cargo, of a material nature other than a human, but both were nearly lost in the natural hazards of the sea. The day previously, when all the travel weary passengers were expecting to disembark and feel the most welcome firmness of the earth beneath them, the ship was becalmed in a dense fog off the coast near Scituate south of Boston. Worse than that, its keel touched the bottom, and the ship was aground for a few hours. But the captain was up to the task by re-balancing the vessel and managing to get it afloat no doubt with the crew running hither and thither under orders and reassuring the bemused of even frightened passengers that all was well and that these things happen from time to time. Once at Boston, the ship was towed to the quarantine harbour where it was then anchored, and the passengers inspected for disease before they travelled the four miles to the city itself. The ship subsequently spent some time in the dry dock where repairs were carried out for the little damage it had received.

And on another occasion when the ship arrived in Liverpool in November 1847, it was not able to dock immediately because it had to stand off in the Mersey due to a storm. It had brought along it with the commercial news and the state of cotton and other crops, and also of the Whig Victory in the election in New York where the democrat James K Polk had been successful. And it brought news of the conflict with Mexico and the states bordering the territories where, fighting against the forces of Santa Anna, US forces backed by expansionist politics were engaged in annexing the Mexican territories of the south west and those bordering the Pacific Ocean. There was still, however, some opposition in the Senate to the annexation of states which yet accepted slavery. Quite soon a violent and destructive civil war would go some way to resolving this issue and some of those emigrants would find themselves out of the frying pan of Europe and into the fire of the New World in America. But by late 1849 the American newspapers, on learning of the conflict of interest between Russia and Turkey in the news brought by the packet ships to their eastern ports, were predicting the outbreak of a general European war. It didn't take long for this to happen and the railway navvies that hadn't yet saved up enough for emigration to those wide open spaces found themselves making railway lines in record breaking time through the Crimea to supply the British army and its allies fighting at Sebastopol. So wherever you went, or if you stayed at home, there would have been a large scale war on your doorstep, if not the very next day, then quite soon after.

The very last cargo discharged from the Ocean Monarch at Liverpool to arrive from Boston consisted of 651 barrels of lard, 12 tierces (tcs as printed) of beef, 22 barrels of mutton, 2 barrels (or bushels) of tongue, 50 packages of coolers and cake oil, and similar quantities of lard, cheese, pork, nearly 19,000 bushels of corn, cotton, tallow, cake oil pressings, cake soap, bread, flour, and oatmeal. It would be the last cargo it would unload. While the excitedly nervous passengers might have taken a moment or two to marvel at the magnificent vessel in which they were soon to embark for a life changing adventure, they would not have known, in their blind confidence and trust, that it would be their coffin. So, the fact that many passengers did die on route due to the harshness of conditions where a frail body might not have the resilience to endure the complete journey, eventually these packet ships loaded with emigrants began to be referred to, with some cynicism, as coffin ships, which more referred to the extreme conditions of the travellers rather that the safety of the ships themselves. The commitment of the passenger and the hopes and belief of a fresh start in a new world over the ocean would perhaps overcome a cynic's caution of, 'Oh, you are travelling in a coffin ship are you? Best of luck'. And most travellers were of a young age, an age from which death cannot be perceived as a reality from which warnings of danger can be dismissed with relative ease and confidence. There were also quite naturally, if painfully so, births on board the ships too. Some of the bodies of the female victims washed ashore after the tragedy were pregnant, and one 'apparently' so while another had given birth, the umbilical cord still being attached when both were collected together off the beach at Bispham. Such is the added burden of the female.

The cargo that it had loaded for this return journey to Boston would be largely salvaged from the bottom of the sea and many of its passengers, hoping for a new life from the desperation of their present situations, would be those lifeless bodies washed ashore on the northwest coasts of England and Wales. The tragedy of the loss of the ship was the sensation of the day and for a short time, elicited the compassion and demonstrated the raw courage of (the generic) man's humanity to man.

The arrival of a ship at a port was perhaps like, in modern times, excitedly waiting for the phone to ring or for the postman to arrive at the door with good news, a letter or a parcel. A ship's most valued cargo, to a broker or a merchant at the time, might be the news they would bring, albeit in the case of America, dependent upon the frequency of arrivals of ships at the port for its freshness, but fresh news nevertheless to those waiting at the dock to hear it officially from the Captain. It did not bring enough news, however to affect the stock markets, news always eagerly awaited by the merchantmen of the town. That would need to arrive on another ship later on. Neither did it bring with it its anchor and chains on this occasion, having parted one and slipped the other off by the NW Lightship, before its arrival in the Mersey, a minor calamity no doubt resolved once in port.

The time lapse in the transmission of news stories, in the days before radio transmissions, would have a direct relevance to the story of the demise of the Ocean Monarch for, while those vessels involved in the rescue which were local, or relatively local, could return to Liverpool with their story the same day or soon after, those vessels which were outward bound, including the Ocean Queen and the New World would not bring back their complete stories until over a month later on their return journey, in which time the self-congratulation and medal distribution of those at home had all been done. The vilification of the New World, one of the major players in the rescue, based on not having a first-hand account or a confused, if evidently honest, account could only be countered by the return of the ship to Liverpool, and its unfortunately and equally vilified Captain Knight, to redeem himself.

But the first person to suffer injury on this voyage of the Ocean Monarch was not a passenger or crew member, but a dock worker, and even before the ship had finished loading. While the ship was lying in the Prince's dock loading its cargo, one of those workers, a chap called Christian Otto slipped and fell into the hold and was severely injured. His was one of many accidents occurring that day. Labour was cheap and there was always another man or boy, ready and willing, and most likely in dire financial need, to take his place.

The cargo would normally take about thirty five working hours to unload (though in August of 1847 it only took thirty three hours to unload) using the journeymen dock workers who would queue up at the beginning of the day, hoping to be taken on for a day's work. Some would work and get paid by the end of the day. Some like Christian Otto would work and might not see the end of the day. While the Health and Safety of today might get ridiculed because of its rigid rules as it's, 'only common sense' to be careful, hazard itself is not prone to a lack of the universality of common sense but has its own rules. In December of the previous year, a fourteen year old boy,

William Fairhurst, was killed when a barrel of turpentine fell onto him as he was unloading the stock from the Ocean Monarch at the Waterloo Dock. On the same day Peter Jordan a sailor from the ship, the General Parkhill, in Prince's Dock, slipped and fell off a plank into the dock and was drowned. And of course the workforce would not all be singing along merrily and getting along famously like a Hollywood musical for the dockworkers, who were mainly Catholic and many being Irish were at loggerheads with the equally numerous carters who were mostly English many being Protestant.

While en route, out in the oceans, the ships could give their position by flag telegraph or be identified by their number or flags as they passed in the nearer of further distance, or even engaging in verbal exchanges if near enough. Each ship arriving in the port would transfer this information to the Exchange news rooms, and which was then reported in the newspapers, under the heading 'spoken to', and in this way the movement of ships could be logged albeit not in real time. Docking at Liverpool on 27th March 1848, the news of the treaty between the USA and Mexico was conveyed inland by the emerging 'electric telegraph' in which the cables were carried on poles along the railway routes for speed and convenience. The news caused a slight movement in Mexican investments on the stock market. The treaty had been signed on February 2nd of that year and fortuitously timed just a week or two before gold had been discovered in the Sacramento valley. Here, with the subsequent demise of the Spanish Missions and their religious and socially cohesive tenets and practices, it was later regretted in some circles that the state of California, now incorporated into the USA by treaty and at the cost of $15m, had turned into a lawless and amoral place by an influx of wealth seekers. But it was a state that didn't sanction slavery and it would not be long before the ships docking in Liverpool would bring news of the turmoil of the Civil War and the subsequent blockades of the cotton exporting ports of the South that would bring the misery of penury to the people of the Lancashire County in which the port of Liverpool was situated. In 1848 these land bound cables carried the news of a policeman, murdered by Chartists in Ashton, back to Liverpool where the suspected murderer was believed to be attempting to flee to America on one of the ships, and thus the Ocean Monarch, as one of those ships at the dockside, had to be searched.

CHARTISTS

Even before the ship had set sail there was drama on board. While there were political fugitives from Ireland taking refuge in Paris and fugitives from France taking refuge in England, and socio-economic fugitives of penury, unemployment and disenfranchisement from Britain getting as far away as possible through emigration, the Ocean Monarch found itself unknowingly the refuge for a suspected Chartist murderer, an Englishman and fugitive from Ashton, a town now in Greater Manchester, itself a city which was a centre of industry containing the artisans and labourers whose physical energies and skills created the wealth of an Empire. It was also a hotbed of Chartist activity, that working class movement which promoted that Charter for better representation of the working class element of the national community. Joseph Radcliffe, (otherwise known as, or stated as Samuel, or James Ratcliffe, or Radcliffe Smith or, at the trial, clearly stated as Joseph Radcliffe) the suspected man in question, had somehow been able to get on board.

It seems that Joseph Radcliffe's father, James, had already booked on the Ocean Monarch before it had become necessary for his son to run away, and the published newspaper lists of the survivors give a James Radcliffe at 22 years of age which could not be Joseph's father since Joseph was in his twenties. It seems that, at some time, Joseph had persuaded his father to include him on the passenger list too and, had he succeeded in doing this, it might have accounted for another of the unnamed passengers along with Alice Wrigley if under a different name. For James Radcliffe to give his son's name as Joseph would not have been considered a very subtle way of running away anonymously so he would be expected to be travelling under a pseudonym and not very subtle if that pseudonym had been James with the same surname. So it is not certain whether Joseph had boarded the vessel under an assumed name or whether he had slipped on unnoticed by anyone, under cover of darkness perhaps.

The murder of course, it has to be considered, was not premeditated but more likely to happen with the depth of resentment and the possession of weapons representing an intent on violence. So it could be imagined that the night in question was only to be a night of macho sabre rattling, violence perhaps being threatened but its extremes not contemplated by most of the assembled mob, so much so that booking in advance to escape justice had not been considered by any of those accused. But when it got serious and a policeman had been murdered in the course of events, the mob dispersed and each member distanced himself from the other, and conveniently found just a few members to rest the accusations upon and this focus whittled down to two and, since one of these felons could not be located, the whole accusation was directed at Joseph Radcliffe.

As for Alice Wrigley there is a James Wrigley from the area involved in the Chartist movement but no evidence has been found to connect him with Alice as husband and wife and it is reported latterly that he had left the year earlier, getting out of the way it could be understood while the going was good, if indeed he was concerned about the inevitable progression towards violence.

1848 itself was the year when the Communist Manifesto was published and Karl Marx from his London base and his friend, Frederick Engels had been meeting at the Red Dragon in Salford since the early 1840's. 1848 was also the year of the Health of Towns Act in which any district that could be called a town would be responsible for cleaning itself up with the provisions of running water, sewerage facilities and the like and, if not, then central Government would become involved demonstrating that change does sometimes originate from the top too, but perhaps not fast enough or fair enough in content for a large part of the disenfranchised national community who were not allowed a say in those decisions.

Communism would be a new word socially and politically, and provisions to clear the squalor of intense overcrowding needed a fresh political approach, and a more immediate solution, and where there was perceived to be no mindset to provide it in that area, it had to be created from the grass roots and this demographic group needed motivating. Where there was no established political desire, the immediacy evident in the grass roots for change, bypassed the eloquence of speech and spilled over into the frustration of incontinent, violent posturing. Direct action was conducted by the frustration of relatively young men with more adrenalin than skills in reasoned argument, to which none had the patience to listen even if they had the desire. Within this frustrated violence which the military were instructed to counter, there were knives and guns and other make-do weapons in several towns and cities in the land, and known Chartist premises where this evident sedition was preached, were raided and the leaders arrested. One lucky joiner, in being badly injured while dismantling the scaffolding after a recent hanging at Liverpool jail, was seen to by a doctor in the prison and he was the nearest doctor available since he was a prisoner there, a Chartist, and one who would no doubt have eloquently spoken for his cause without considering violence. Lots of folk were arrested, which included vicars, as their socialist views from pulpits or pedestals, however correct and noble, nevertheless proved to disrupt the stability of society, and change was considered secondary to the protection of the status quo by the self-interest of those in power.

Joseph Radcliffe was a Chartist leader and was on the police radar for being part of a proactive group, styled the Ashton National Guard who preferred this direct kick-ass action rather than discussion and intellectual argument, as was the original design of the first, organised working class movements. The mission statement of the movement was to demand representation in Parliament through granting franchise and the demand for better working conditions. An infiltrator to the group however, a Robert Emmet and employed by the police, reported that this group in Ashton was hell bent to 'fire houses, railway premises or anything.' Once the name of Robert Emmet became public knowledge he was harassed and beaten up and his wife received death threats. A bit like being a modern football (soccer) referee where the fanaticism of misplaced loyalty assassinates a proper balance of reason. Robert Emmet and his family had to be removed for safety's sake further away into Manchester.

The commitment to violence for the cause was demonstrated at 11pm on the 14th August when a group of about fifty armed men marched down Bentinck Street in Ashton under Lyne. There was nothing secretive about it as clogs or hobnailed boots on cobbles would have made quite a loud and threatening noise. Perhaps they had been encouraged by the fact that the military from the town garrison had been depleted in numbers by their requirement in Ireland. They marched in column two abreast, some had guns and other weapons, all carrying makeshift pikes on their right shoulders. Dreaming of a nationwide insurrection, similar to the Parisian blockades of February earlier in the year, in every town they were evidently bent on violence and destruction. Samuel Smith, who was not a policeman at the time but had been, and would be one again after the incident, and his wife were indoors when they heard the noisy activity in the street and were suspicious enough not only to open a curtain like a curious neighbour, but to go out and find out what was happening. In Bentinck Street, at the corner of Moss Street, they were confronted by a group of men one of who was named Samuel Sigley and who put a gun to Samuel Smith's head and violently advised him to, 'Go away from that woman, or I will blow your bloody brains out.' Fortunately for Samuel Smith there was a member of the group called James Milligan who possessed a little more reason than raw, loaded passion, and who knocked the gun away from the threatened victim and who advised him categorically though with threat, without wanting to kill him, to go away or join forces with the ranks of armed men.

Samuel Smith and his wife returned home safe, and it is to be considered that the armed men did not know that he had once been a police officer or he might have met the same fate as Joseph Bright a little later on. The police were not liked. They were in the way of the exercise and expression of violence. Samuel Smith himself, after going home, and naturally inquisitive, left the house once more to investigate and shortly later heard a shot and a female scream. It was a shot which was probably the one that had killed Joseph Bright.

After encountering Samuel Smith and his wife, the men had continued on. Marching in column and only a little further on by Brooke Street they were alarmed when they were advised that a policeman was on his way and so they turned to meet him, confronting him in the same way as they had earlier confronted Samuel Smith and his wife. Joseph Bright the policeman in question, knew some of the men and thought he had a better rapport with them and believed he could reason with the men better than the constable that had originally been put on his beat and whose place he had taken. Unfortunately he was wrong. The men manhandled him and dragged him forcibly down Bentinck Street and, while he tried to ingratiate himself with them some of who he knew, his pleas were ignored. It was alleged that one man pierced him with the blade of a pike and another, less bloodthirsty man, had tried to divert the thrust of the pike way from the policeman. Joseph Bright had tried to defend himself by instinctively grabbing the blade and, as it pierced his thigh, he stooped and someone, allegedly Joseph Radcliffe, but never determined or proved, fired the gun into his chest which killed him after his last, pleading words of 'Spare my life!' Knowing some of the young lads by name who were attacking him he had thought himself quite safe. But he had to die, like the peaceful archbishop at the Parisian barricades he was in the way, an obstacle to the fulfilment of violence. The gunshot awoke some of the people behind the doors and curtains in the street and those doors and curtained windows opened to reveal many subsequent witnesses. The armed group in the street immediately disappeared in a confused state now no longer inspired, justified and lauded revolutionaries like a Garibaldi had been in the streets of London, but cold blooded murderers in the eyes of anyone around them. Those slumbering indoors woken by the noise, opened their windows and doors too and came out of their houses. James Gray the landlord of the Red Lion and some other men carried the profusely bleeding body of the policeman indoors to the pub. It was too late. He was dead, killed with that single bullet.

Policeman as guardians of the law and order of the society in which the armed men were objecting to might be seen as the enemy. Constable Henry Taylor had been on duty and when he had heard a commotion down Bentinck Street had gone into the middle of the road to see what it was all about. Perhaps a mistake since he was spotted by a group of men who immediately charged at him with the rather crude but vengeful rallying cry of, 'That's the bastard. After him!' (The newspaper prints it as 'b———-'). Constable Taylor took flight and escaped and was able to give evidence at the later trial in December. Meanwhile Joseph Radcliffe found he had blood on his jacket (referred to as a 'swinger' jacket) so he swapped it for the moleskin one of one his conspirators, a chap called Winterbottom, and made his escape staying at Winterbottom's house with a couple of other conspirators for a few days until he could make a complete escape. There was nowhere to hide in England and the vast expanses of America beckoned via the imminent departure of any ship at the dockside in Liverpool.

So, at the time that the Ocean Monarch was due to sail, in late August, warrants for the arrests of seventeen members of the Chartist movement under an indictment for various acts of sedition and 'treasonable conspiracy' or aiding and abetting the same, had been issued at the Liverpool assizes. Joseph Radcliffe, considered to be a Chartist leader in Ashton was one of those members fearing arrest as the group who maintained their revolutionary dreams and intentions of armed conflict against oppression. After preliminary investigation, Joseph Radcliffe had been directly implicated in the murder of the policeman in Ashton and he became a wanted man. Eventually leaving the Ashton region, he managed to get on board the Ocean Monarch hoping to return to America where, it is reported, he had been before with other Chartist members after the general strike of 1842. However, long before the murderer Dr Crippen had been the first to be arrested by the telegraph message across the Atlantic Ocean, all the names of the men implicated in the proscribed group of the 'Ashton National Guard' were relayed by telegraph overland from Manchester to Liverpool and back, and seventeen men were arrested and bailed on the same night. Joseph Radcliffe had been traced to Liverpool and the police scoured the passenger lists. They already had more than a suspicion that the America bound ship was a reasonable place to look for any potential fugitives, since it afforded a rational means of escape with its imminent departure. This search by the police was referred to during the inquest on the demise of the ship when, with some mild alarm and veiled criticism, it was observed that the police had been in the hold searching its dingy and dark interiors with lighted candles as they attempted to track down potential fugitives. When Joseph Radcliffe had been aware of two policeman boarding the ship to look for and arrest him, he immediately ran to hide among the crates, where he hoped he wouldn't be found. He had covered himself with straw and timbers hoping to be fully concealed, but the light of the policeman's candle reflected off the nails of his boots and gave him away. He might have thought that bad luck was his bed partner on this occasion for the departure of the Ocean Monarch had been delayed a day or two by poor weather which had given the police more time. His sentence of death would come later, though commuted and, unlike his potential fellow passengers, he would have a long life ahead of him. But fortune had really favoured him, for many of those innocents on the Ocean Monarch the death sentence in the guise of misfortune had already been delivered and could not be commuted. Once arrested he was first taken to Liverpool, then over to Ashton for trial, and then back to Liverpool Kirkdale and the Bridie gaol since, like many of the artisan workers arrested at the same time, he couldn't come up with the sureties for the bail.

There was a great crowd outside the courthouse in Chester in December for the eventual trial, and the police and the military had to be out in force in attendance. There were also ten men who had been arrested in Bradford, and who were implicated in the murder of policeman Bright and whose trial had been adjourned until this date.

In London also, thirty one men were on trial 'for feloniously compassing the levying of war against her Majesty the Queen'. They were bound over in the sum £100 (£8,101.13p) each before the full trial at the Central Criminal Court and, if they couldn't come up with the surety, they would have to wait in prison for their trial. For Joseph Radcliffe, ultimately, having been arrested on the ship and later tried, he was sentenced to death, his wife sobbing in the courtroom while the sentence was pronounced though the jury recommended mercy. However, as it was never proven that Joseph Radcliffe had fired the gun, his sentence was commuted to prison and then transportation – with a banishment from ever returning to his home country. But he did, like Magwitch the convict in Dickens' Great Expectations, though he didn't stay for, having made good, it was only en route from Australia to San Francisco the place where he ended his days in relative close proximity, perhaps ironically so, to that famous hero of the Ocean Monarch rescues, a very real life saver in Frederick Jerome, not an alleged life taker, and who had also made his home in the same Californian city.

For Joseph, if he had thought he had been a bit of a loser from the moment he had concealed himself within the freight of the Ocean Monarch, ultimately that bad luck would be his salvation. Had the ship sailed with him, it was odds on, though unknown to him hiding in the holds and less aware of an emergency, that he would lose his life anyway. But if he could have realised the acute danger then, he would have been in the unravelling of the tragedy, and any genuineness in his commitment to humanity would have been put to the test in the tragic events that followed if he had had to put his own life in danger for the sake of others. Perhaps he would have been proved a hero, and saved a life rather than allegedly have taken one. Or perhaps he would have been proved a villain once more and ignored the desperate pleas of others less fortunate than himself. If he hadn't been arrested, he might not have had the full life that he was reportedly to enjoy as a consequence.

The man called Sigley and who was equally involved in the affair and the murder had managed somehow, to abscond to America. It is not known how the seemingly inveterately violent man, had allegedly absconded to America as was believed at the trial, though he had had some assistance from his aunt in lending him clothes and possibly money. Perhaps he had at first thought of boarding the Ocean Monarch along with Joseph Radcliffe, but it seems, it transpires, that he settled in New England and, though in New Jersey, it wasn't that far away in American travel terms to Massachusetts also in New England where was settled that other hero of the Ocean Monarch rescues, Jotham Bragdon. And he was unpopularly outspoken on the anti-slavery side. Perhaps making amends and doing penance for his earlier inhumane actions in Ashton.

Both Joseph Radcliffe and Samuel Sigley made good and led long and fruitful lives it would seem. For the judge at their trial to claim that universal suffrage was a useless concept was the sentiment of a privileged man with a limited perception of others. The manufacturing working population of Britain would continue to struggle and achieve just that until the later 20th century and early 21st century showed that comfort and complacency and a shifting in the content in the working classes would eventually bring an ironic truth to the judge's words as the natural cause of self-preservation in the human individual embraces the right wing position of politics.

For those who didn't want to get involved in insurrection, there was always emigration, for it was from this oppression that the skilled and semi-skilled artisan and families, with no democratic recognition in their own country, would want to escape to the freedom and wide open spaces of the New World, be it America, Canada, New Zealand or Australia or anywhere with established British interests where land was available for a price, and a belief of freedom available with the nerve to travel. Many of those with that objective who sailed on the Ocean Monarch on August 24th 1848 would not see those dreams or ambitions realised.

But life always throws out ironies and there is a twist in the tale of emigration in this story where those accused in the Chartist trial and who had been encouraged to turn Queen's evidence against their former friends were given free passage to Australia to start a new life. While both Joseph Radcliffe and Samuel Sigley it appears, both involved, but not murderously so it was believed by the court and then convicted and sentenced, ultimately led what appear to be decent lives, the real and unidentified murderers themselves were granted that free passage by the Emigration Commission and arrived in the wide open spaces of Australia that many innocents could only dream of. Perhaps a greater justice might have seen them on the Ocean Monarch instead when the innocent dreams of many were wiped out by having the misfortune of being in the wrong place at the wrong time.

THE DISCOVERY OF THE FIRE AS THE TRAGEDY UNFOLDS

Having arrived in Liverpool from Boston on 27th July 1848, the Ocean Monarch left Liverpool at 5am on Thursday the 24th August to make the return trip across the Atlantic. The ship was commissioned, not chartered and it had a large contingent of paying passengers. Those friends and family who had visited the passengers on the ship had left their family members or acquaintances on board the evening before the early morning of departure. Unbeknown to those friends, families and acquaintances, after making their farewells and staying in the busy port for a while before making the journey home, they would soon have had the unpleasant and often heart breaking task of identifying some of the bodies in the dead house, or were at a later date, to drag out the pain of losing someone close by an obligation to be present at the inquest. James Tierney, a labourer from Omagh and at present living in Liverpool had identified the body of his mother, Ellen, in the dead house. Johanna Tobin, one of the rescued, that of her sister Mary, with whom she had been a passenger on the ship. She had two sisters with who she was travelling. Her other sister Honora was also saved though it is Johanna the younger who it is reported as dealing with the identification of the deceased sister Mary afterwards. It seems that the sisters were from Cork in Ireland. At this first inquest of the first bodies, were those also of Geoffrey Fynch, fifteen month old Elisabeth Hatherton, and an unidentified seven year old boy. But they were the first of many bodies and represented the tragedies of many, many more.

Having been escorted out of the dock, the Ocean Monarch passed the Formby lightship at 7am and discharged the Mersey pilot, the steam tug that had guided it out into the open sea at 8am, once past the Bell buoy. Had the steam tug stayed around a short a time longer, it could have been the means of saving many more lives and there might have been minimal casualties if any at all. But the human being is not privileged to possess the power of prescience. The ship's company consisted of the Captain, James Murdoch, thirty four hands including one boy, and there were two carpenters, two mates, three stewards, a cook and the ship's surgeon. Included in the passenger list were nine first cabin, seventeen second cabin and 'about' three hundred and thirty steerage passengers in two compartments, front and rear. Various quoted totals don't always add up but, with the 'four other' passengers who are not named and who would include Alice Wrigley, then the total would reach just short of four hundred however it is calculated. The ship also carried a cow and several sheep for fresh milk and meat and their screams of pain and fear could be heard in the midst of the tragedy as they slowly burnt to death confined in their tethers. The cargo, in crates stuffed with flammable straw, was stored in various parts of the ship. Along with the passage money all this cargo amounted to £2,600 (£311,519).

The elder son and grandson of that former, naval seaman who was shipwrecked off Capetown in 1799 when the HMS Sceptre went down, left from Liverpool for New York in 1849 almost a year after the tragedy of the Ocean Monarch, the dreams of freedom there in the New World for many of the émigrés put on hold a little more than a decade later when the army of the south began to threaten the city in its march northwards during the Civil War. This being the fate of many of these immigrants who survived the transatlantic crossing, his own grandson wasn't one who could have afforded to pay his way out of conscription like those few privileged folk who could do so. Also in Liverpool at the time was a family in the confectionary trade in Liverpool and who also, through marriage, would be connected to the old seafarer's family in the following generations. The products of this baking trade of theirs were hopefully not contaminated with foreign substances, as much was in the Victorian bakery business, but cakes and buns would be in high demand the following year to feed the crowds who flocked to the events held to raise money for the survivors of the Ocean Monarch.

There was a large contingent of Irish passengers on the ship, many of who would be escaping from the effects of the Great Hunger, the famine that had decimated the nation, and possibly others from the threat of imprisonment or execution for an association with the Young Ireland rebellion of that year and yet more who had been expelled from their meagre homes as they were in the way of the landowners plans for expansion of land use. There was also travelling amongst them, the wife and child of a bank robber, hoping to meet up in the New World, but they never did. The Irish passengers were contained in the rear of the ship and the English in the forward part. There was the difference of religion too, Catholic on one side and Protestant on the other, and the two nationalities who were largely identified the one with the other religion, would perhaps look at each other with the suspicion of scepticism or condescension, sentiments that might soon be dispelled among the burning timbers and the uncompromising seas as their supplicant prayers to the same God who would nevertheless allow some to live and some to die whatever their nationality and however they perceived that Godhead. 1848 was the year that the British Government was reading the 'Reconciliation of the Pope of Rome Bill', a potential reconciliation that positively disgusted the hardliners. But little of this would matter as raw humanity was expressed in the rescue of survivors from the imminence of death. There is no record of anyone asking the religion of another before rescuing them.

Perhaps some of the émigrés had heard of the gold that had been discovered in the Sierra Nevada and the Sacramento valley of California in January of that year and dreamed of prosperity and a better future. Though they were travelling to a free country, it was nevertheless a country which accepted slavery in many parts of it, and there was a growing dissatisfaction especially in the North though, even here, the Liberals were dragging their feet, stalling from a commitment to tackle its existence and it was a dissatisfaction that resulted in the formation of the breakaway Free Soil party a couple of years earlier. One of the self-sacrificing heroes of the Ocean Monarch's rescue attempts would be involved in the Union navy and be captured and put in chains during the savagery of the Civil War that followed a little more than a decade or so after the destruction of the Ocean Monarch. The émigrés were moving into the freedom of space but, once populated by the human being, this space would eventually prove to be as dangerous and constricted as the limited spaces in the lives that they had left behind.

Of the married females on board, some wives were alone, and other wives with young families were going out to meet husbands and families already out there, and some were pregnant carrying the next generation within them. Alice Wrigley had, it seems, been on her way to join her husband who had reportedly left for Boston the year before. Some were complete families of husbands, wives and children and other relatives, most of a young age as the passenger lists reveal.

The ships weren't entirely on their own in the vast ocean during the long journey to and from the busy port of Liverpool. The passage of any vessel was habitually recorded by telegraph to the Exchange Rooms in Liverpool until out of sight. From then on identifying numbers and flags would be spotted by other vessels and continually updated on their journey as other ships passed them by and recorded in the captain's log. Tragically the Ocean Monarch had only reached as far as Abergele Bay in between the Great Orme Head and Abergele in North Wales when in sight of the telegraph facility on the Orme Head. Just into the third tack with the order to 'bout ship!' echoed across its decks to change its course from heading inland and keep its direction to the open sea, a fire was discovered below decks about mid-day. The ship was about five or six miles off shore, and soon smoke could be observed by helpless eyes from the Welsh shore without the detail of the intimate tragedies unfolding.

The catastrophe that befell the Ocean Monarch was transmitted in more detail by flag signal from the telegraph station on the Great Orme Head to the Exchange News Rooms at Liverpool. With his 'glass', his telescope, the telegraph officer would be able to see, from the advantageous height of his position, several ships in the busy shipping lane, the two full, square rigged ships leaving Liverpool, the Ocean Monarch for Boston and its sister ship the New World bound for New York. The maligned American mail ship Cambria and also the steamship Orion, both of who it had been claimed had not bothered to stop at all and give assistance, reflected as a coincidence of similar nature in the tragedy of the Titanic over fifty years later, would also be in his sights, and the coastal traffic consisting of the steam ship, the City of Dublin's Company, steamer Prince of Wales, the later but significant arrival of the Liverpool built Brazilian naval, steam frigate, Dom Afonso and the fore and aft sails of the smaller boats, the yacht, Queen of the Ocean, the pilot boat and occasional fishing smack all involved in the rescue operation. Nothing would have seemed out of place at the time until the smoke was observed pouring out of one of the ships in his sights. But the full tragedy of the event was not known until the first of the passing vessels, drawn into the event by both the written and unwritten maritime law and the compassion for others in difficulty at sea, arrived back at Liverpool with some survivors on board, and conveyed the news. The accuracy of the reporting from the telegraph post was given great credit at the time, a message reaching Liverpool in about twelve seconds, but the full extent of the tragedy was not known until 5.30pm when the Queen of the Ocean arrived back at the port. On the BBC series Coast, an experiment between this method of flag signalling and the modern mobile phone came out as equal in time taken, about twelve seconds to reach Liverpool.

The first message received at the telegraph office in Liverpool to where all the journalists hurried was read as, 'A ship on fire. Has the letter T on her fore topsail. Outward bound. Her number, per chart, 163. A steamer bearing down towards her. Her main and mizzen masts are gone.' So already, before any help could arrive, the fire had taken a firm grip of the ship in its centre and at the rear. The telegraph wasn't able to determine any detail and it was hoped that there would be no casualties, but the human tragedy that unfolded was only conveyed by the survivors and those on the rescue ships much later in the day. The last communication from the telegraph on the incident was at 7pm when it could report that the ship had finally sunk.

It was never firmly established how the fire actually started or who was or were responsible, and the accounts of the survivors can be conflicting, while providing a scene of utter terror and confusion which had tried its best to bury the truth. The packed front end of the ship as represented in the eyewitness sketches and subsequent paintings show a great mass of folk crammed together at this point. There would have been pressure from those closest to the fire to push those in front of them ever more forward until there was nowhere left to go but into the uninviting sea. Eventually the bowsprit, the furthermost part of the ship forward, collapsed with the weight of those who were desperately clinging to it.

But, in the beginning, once the shout of 'fire!' had been given, a concern which soon turned to panic, gripped the passengers and confused the crew because the seat of the alleged fire took some minutes to locate. These minutes were too long for the nervous passengers and pandemonium broke out almost immediately as all sense of order was lost. The lower decks where the bulk of the payload of human beings was accommodated and the stairways up from the lower decks to the light and the fresh air were soon congested with folk fleeing for their lives with nowhere safe to go, rescuing what belongings they could as they fled.

In the quiet composure of the courtroom at the later enquiry and, even later, across the benches in Parliament, it was generally understood that the culprit was a steward aboard the ship, the same steward who had discovered the fire and went straight to inform the captain who had immediately ordered an investigation. Though the steward was easiest to blame, a satisfactory explanation resting on reasonable conjecture, but not proof, could only be contrived as all other considerations were excluded. The fire was at the rear of the ship and some way below the captain's cabin, the points being connected by an air vent and it was a relatively short distance for the steward to rush in a mild panic and trust that the captain would sort everything out. But before the fire was made evident to the captain some of the passengers were already aware of it and, before any sense of order could be constructed, a fear and a panic shot through the ship faster than any fire could take hold. From then on it was chaos and many people had their own version of events which often conflicted and equally often complied.

Jotham (referred to as John or Jonathan in some reports) Bragdon the first mate on the Ocean Monarch and, later on, Frederick Jerome of the New World would be the main players in the extensive and prolonged rescue attempts at the cutting edge of the tragedy. Jotham being first mate aboard the Ocean Monarch when the fire started and Frederick Jerome arriving some time later through the desperate proceedings, from the New World packet ship, and he was the major player in the finale when, after three agonising hours of both success and failure, there were cheers of relief and congratulation for the last, living person off the burning ship after so many had previously perished.

In the very beginning, before the alarm began and the panic filled the decks and the holds, and before the passengers and crew realised they were on a burning ship which might as well have been a bonfire because there was nowhere to run to get away from it because all around them ironically perhaps was water, Jotham Bragdon was at the front of the ship on his way to tack, as an adjustment in direction was now relevant. It was a regular part of his job and he was probably diverted in his thoughts by the contentment of returning home to Boston and to his wife. Their son had been born in the same year so he would have least been aware of his wife's pregnancy if their son had not already been born before this date so there was plenty for him to look forward to. But, whatever spare space he had in his mind in the automatic nature of the task in hand of his profession, there was none of this space left for casual thought when he came across people shouting 'fire!!'. Immediately, the instincts and obligations of his profession took over and he instead concentrated his thoughts and focussed his attention in a hurried and concerned diversion to see the source of the alleged concern. In his professional mind, there was probably no real concern at first, assuming it to be a passenger's lapse, an event which could easily be controlled and extinguished, and it could only be one of their kind who could have had ignored the strict rules concerning fire. Even before the fire, in a preventative measure issued by the Captain, he had gone among all the passengers warning them of the dangers of fire and that smoking was strictly forbidden.

His story is perhaps the most accurate and true, but there are many other stories that come out of the incident and which vary in their accuracy due to the state of panic or expectation of the responsibilities of those in who the varying status of passengers or crew had put their trust. As the first mate, he was influential throughout the incident. Prompted by the fearful shout of 'fire!!' he was one of the first at the very beginning to find a source of the fire due to the excessive heat curling out of an air vent in the after state cabin at about 12 noon. Once he had located the very real flames below he immediately called for help and a supply of water and opened the ventilator, also removing some flooring in the cabin. By this time, the passengers below deck were already in a panic and were rushing and screaming here and there in utter confusion as the fire had been discovered by their accommodation. It had taken about twenty minutes to get to the stage of pouring water down the vent and the hole in the floor but the fire was already well advanced as it was eagerly eating through the slender, softwood of the white deal timbers that made up the passenger accommodations. It soon proved impossible to put the fire out as the water turned to steam and created a dense smoke and the firefighters were forced back up on deck. From then on there were only two options available to every person on board the ship, and they were either to remain on board and hope for rescue from another ship, or abandon the ship altogether. To the despair of many, the lifeboats as it turned out were blatantly not much of an option.

One of the passengers that he might have passed in his attempt to get to the source of the fire at first was Johanna Tobin. She was just one of these alarmed passengers who had to act immediately. There was only one decision to make, and that was to get away from the fire or the smoke, which was beginning to spread through the vessel, and follow others who looked like they knew what to do or knew what was going on. She had been sat on a box in the steerage along with her sisters Mary and Honora when they heard the shouts of fire and they were among the numerous passengers and crew who immediately ran up to the deck to find out what was going on. Whether the sisters were able to return below decks to retrieve any valuables, which might not have amounted to much, is not known but when it was their turn to take the rope down into the rescue boats, when these eventually arrived, her thirty eight year old sister Mary went down the rope before her. It appears that she had slipped off the rope and into the unforgiving sea and was swept away from the generous and willing arms of the rescuers, for it was the last time Johanna saw her alive. She identified her sister's body at the inquest and took her for burial from the dead house at the docks. Johanna remained on the ship to the end and was one of the last to be rescued from the fore part of the ship by one of the small boats that came alongside the ship. Her sister Honora Tobin is mentioned alongside both Mary and Johanna in the passenger lists but she is not mentioned further. But she was possibly rescued along with Johanna who was reportedly rescued by Jotham Bragdon, Frederick Jerome and a small party of resilient sailors of differing ranks, in charge of the oars of the small boats in the choppy seas.

Meanwhile on the evidence of the second mate, William Percy Gibbs, seeking the source of the fire through the smoke, as he went aft of the ship, he came across Jotham Bragdon and at what appeared to be the source. He immediately began helping, now with the captain's knowledge and acquiescence, to cut a hole in the lower deck in order to pour down water into it. But this initial effort was hampered because even with the aid of a swiftly organised chain of buckets, the water pumps could not fill the buckets fast enough to supply the men with a sufficient amount of water. It would have been a hot job but feasible with the notion that the fire could be contained, brought under control and put out at that time but, when it was no longer possible to remain in the smoke and the heat, the men left their bucket chain and went up on deck. It took only about fifteen minutes for flames to burst though the skylight in front of the mizzen mast at the rear and they soon took hold of the mast itself. It was now out of control and the options available were to either remain on the burning ship and wait in hope for rescue, or leave the ship and put the trust in the unforgiving waters of the sea. From somewhere the order was heard to immediately clear the boats. The stern boat had already caught fire. With the second option of being burnt to death on the taffrail at the rear of the ship, the first option was patently to lower one of the boats, an exercise which was accomplished in a hurry but in such a hurry that only three crew and three passengers could scramble into it without waiting for anyone else to arrive through the flames. This boat managed to escape and reach eventual safety with its lucky few passengers. The second boat to be lowered into the water was poorly prepared, and with a single oar only, the boat with its light load drifted helplessly away from the ship though still attached to it by a rope which then provided the means for many more to descend into the sea in an attempt to reach its relative safety. Seeing this boat in trouble Jotham Bragdon had eventually to decide whether to stay on the ship and see what he could do for those on board or watch helplessly as a second tragedy might unfold if that boat were to capsize and make itself unserviceable thus denying others the chance of escape. He could stay or jump but, for this moment, he decided to stay as there was work to do on board despite its immediate dangers to himself and, as his story unfolds, it was a decision that would save the lives of many, attributable to him.

Meanwhile, the Captain, both aggrieved and probably embarrassed to be losing his ship to a fire, was quick to blame the passengers. While the cook, a 'coloured' man, had been able to get down the rope and into the waiting boat, it wasn't so much race but socio-economics that separated one human being from another. White as a race was numerically superior in the western world but the working classes and the poor were growing in number, influence and power and hence were beginning to constitute a threat to the established order. Those of low level social status within the Irish and English lower working classes, even though they comprised of skilled artisans that made up most of the steerage passengers, the cheapest, packed and most confined of accommodation on the vessel, were no doubt the ones that had, by their ignorance, started the fire. It couldn't have been any other way to those of the perceived superiority of social status. The Captain had confiscated smoking pipes (or the dudheens of the Irish contingent) but he doesn't claim that he had confiscated the lucifer matches that were used to create a flame. Some of these were found aflame in one of the survivor's pockets, even though he was soaked to the skin as he was hauled out of the sea aboard one of the boats. So either one of these 'low level' human beings (who the Christian God had stricken with severe famine, squalor and poverty in Ireland or just poverty and squalor and a little bit of starvation in England) would had to have been guilty of starting it either by a sneaky smoke among the crates of china, packed with protective (and highly combustible) straw, or starting a fire by an air vent which in their naivety was mistaken for a chimney. This appears to be the sentiment of Captain Murdoch, in grabbing at reasons, in the subsequent inquest and the crew, and at least one cabin passenger, stood by him and exonerated him from any blame. If found guilty he would have been charged with manslaughter. At the subsequent inquest one of the sailors confirmed that that they were not allowed to smoke below decks but occasionally went up on deck to have a smoke 'on the sly'. This seemed to be confirmed by the fact that a seaman named Jenkins had been seen below decks in the Lazeretto, as the sick room was called, with a lighted candle. It was also observed that he had returned on deck without the candle but claimed he had put it in his pocket in order to grease his boots later, an excuse perhaps, but an indication that naturally the rules were not always adhered to.

Joshua Wilson, a passenger who didn't like the captain, in a statement says that he was on deck watching the mate hand out tobacco to the crew, so smoking on board, if it couldn't be entirely prevented, could at least be subject to strict controls. Suddenly as he was observing this tobacco hand-out, there was a cry of 'fire'. Buckets, if they could be found, were in scant supply he complained.

During the panic the conduct of the captain as stated by some of the surviving witnesses, who were perhaps contemptuous of the class of folk perceived to be above them and wanted to blame them, was that of an irascible character and one that had no time for his human payload. It was reported that he swore and cursed contemptuously at the panicking passengers. One man even claimed that he had heard the captain declare himself no longer the captain because the ship was on fire and that it had to be every man for himself. On the reported evidence, in the Manchester Courier, of John Bell, a machine maker who lived at 13 Water Street Manchester, and whose wife, Emma had been drowned, he was unashamed to give his evidence claiming that the captain behaved like a brute and in one instance, even before the fire, told another passenger, the same Joshua Wilson it seems, to throw his child overboard because it was crying and making a noise. During the panic of the fire, he claimed that the captain did not do enough and didn't even seem to care about the safety of the passengers. He also claimed that there were several ships standing off but none appeared to be offering any kind of help. As this was not the case by the evidence of other sources, John Bell's evidence might suggest that even though it didn't appear that he liked the captain, and the captain didn't like the steerage passengers, swearing at them at any given opportunity, as several avowed to the fact, his evidence was perhaps somewhat prejudicial. Perhaps for Joshua Wilson, the despair of losing both his wife and his child before his eyes, he needed to blame whoever and whatever he could. Edward Jones, a farmer from Irlam, who had lost his wife on the ship, also corroborated John Bells' account. But whether the captain was the nicest man on earth or the worst, some opinions were loaded, and there was little the captain could do in the situation at the time and was perhaps understandably unable to give a definitive answer to all the many questions of 'what can be done?' that were being fired at him from all sides. The more complete story comes out at the subsequent inquest where Captain Murdoch, with his solicitors at his side, is able to tell his own version of events.

In another account, the fire was claimed to have originated from near the steering wheel, so it couldn't have been the passengers who were the guilty parties and the claims and counter claims could no longer be verified. Within the many theories of how and where and when the fire broke out, is another and that it was that the cook and the stewardess who were using a candle instead of a lamp in the spirit store and the combustible nature of those fumes in the store caused the ignition. The cook and the stewardess were described as 'coloured'. The occupation of stewardess, 'coloured' or not, was often intimated at the time as being a euphemism for hooker and there for the sexual favours to complement the wage, or the wage to complement the income, if any, from sexual favours. In most cases this would be a necessary reluctance on the part of any stewardess.

It was in the days when it was convenient to blame the Irish, or the lower intelligence of the English working class for anything that went wrong. 'Coloured' people were another element of the emerging mix of human society who would have their day to be conveniently blamed for everything. The stewardess, who is never given a name, knowing that there was powder stored on the ship lost her life by being overcome by the fumes as she tried to remove the 20 pounds or so (reports differ between 20 and 25 pounds; 9-11 kilos) of powder that was in danger of exploding. Rushing in to remove it, and I guess to throw it overboard where it could be rendered harmless, she was beaten back by the smoke and though she managed to regain the deck, she unfortunately died there, presumably of smoke inhalation. Had she made it back with the gunpowder through her quick thinking, devotion to duty and heroism she would have been in line to receive the twenty guineas (about £2,500 today) reward that was presented to Mr Whiston Bristow by Lloyds of London, a cabin passenger on the ship, who had heroically been able to succeed in doing this and, by preventing an explosion, had been able to save many lives. Other reports state that the powder did go off but was not in a confined enough space to do much damage. Such is the confusion of reported events.

The ship's surgeon, William Ellis claimed that the fire had broken out in a cabin and is full of praise for the Captain who stood his ground to the last. Mr Ellis, after jumping into the water was picked up by the boat from the Ocean Monarch, in which the mate, Jotham Bragdon was eventually in charge. He had lost everything he owned, all his equipment, his books and his diploma from the Royal College of Surgeons. But his sweetheart hadn't lost him, since he was a survivor, and he later married on the 14th November to Mary Corrigan, daughter of the late J Corrigan Esq. He states that he was taken to a fishing smack from Wexford and put on board there before being delivered to Liverpool. There were many vessels in the vicinity of the burning ship, which are named in some newspaper articles and not in others, in the confusion of the events and the contemporary accounts connected to it.

But wherever the fire had started, and however the ignition was caused, smoke was soon plainly evident coming from the rear of the ship. To those of the passengers however who were lying down due to sea sickness in the depths and the murkiness of the steerages it was not as evident at first, and their subsequent ignorant panic and confusion deafened their ears to the captain's pleas. It is understandable that the captain might have reverted to some maritime language, unbefitting to the captain's table among his cabin guests, when his instructions were not understood or plainly ignored in the confusion and the need to survive. Many were running around in wild panic and confusion, and in this way many children became separated from their parents. Children were pushed out of the way and lost in the confusion as the need to survive overtook the care for others and the morality attached to that sentiment. Many folk were described as being naked (or as naked as can be) as they had been lying on their bunks having succumbed to sea sickness. A polite sense of Victorian nakedness would have meant that if just some of the many hundreds of clothes worn were removed, it would still leave many hundred still covering the person, but few enough to constitute a demure idea of nakedness.

Some of these people amidst this panic would live and some would die. Some would die with their clothes on. Some would die with their clothes off. Some would die because of the default selfishness of others, and some would live only because of the heroic selflessness of others. A frightened crowd hemmed in the captain if not beseeching him to save them, then berating him for letting his ship burn, but inattentive to his pleas to stay calm as help could be seen approaching. After all he was the man in charge, his skills and experience should be able to overrule their naiveties and fears.

It was self-evident that other vessels were in the vicinity, and they would be their salvation, he assured them. But panic overrode even a miniscule portion of hope or belief. Men, women and children were running around in a haphazard manner screaming and shouting. Some of those who returned below decks to retrieve belongings were smothered in the dense smoke and died there.

When the direction of the wind had cancelled the option of running as close to landfall as possible which was the Captain's initial objective and instruction, the anchor had been dropped and the sails changed once more to keep the ship stationary and into the wind as soon as it was evident that the fire was at the rear of the ship and the wind blowing down the deck from front to back would help to keep it there for a long as possible, and sufficiently long enough to enable the approaching vessels to reach them and effect a rescue. The captain had work to do to save his ship. He couldn't stand around purely as an advisor and comforter.

But there was little that the captain could do that was fully correct. By now despairing of any sort of order, but relying on his expertise, when the anchors had to be dropped to keep the ship stationary, there were tragically several passengers crammed haphazardly around the anchor chains and the gearing there and, when the chains were released it caused several women and children who were seated by the cable, to be crushed or somehow dragged into the water where presumably most would have been lost. They perhaps thought they had felt safe there. It would have been out of the way of the panicking passengers running around wildly, everyone for themselves, dragging their boxes onto the deck and opening them taking out anything of value if indeed there was anything of value to take out, and stuffing them into their clothing about their persons.

The flag of distress, the upturned jack, had been raised at the front of the ship to alert the telegraph and any other vessels in the vicinity that might be able to afford assistance.

The serious nature of the distress would now be quite evident now that the midsection of the ship was aflame and the panicking passengers continued to provide a scene of complete chaos uncontrollable by captain or crew. Most crowded to the front of the ship but many were observed on the poop deck, perhaps being the highest part it might have been thought they were safe enough by being at the furthest possible distance from the conflagration. The heat was intense, clothes were thrown off without the shame of embarrassment. Two of the four boats carried by the ship were burnt in the conflagration as there was allegedly no crew to lower them so the ship had only two serviceable escape boats and these had already been lowered by those who thought they could make a quick escape sometimes without a thought for others. These two boats had been hurriedly and carelessly lowered overboard and only those near at hand were able to get into these. Orders were ignored due to the panic of the exigencies of survival. Both boats, one of which was undersubscribed as there was plenty of space for more folk in it, the other in danger of being oversubscribed as the amount of people attempting to get in to it would have swamped it. This latter boat was being pulled by its connecting rope towards the gangway by the desperate passengers on the deck wanting to get into it. It was then that Jotham Bragdon took decisive action and jumped into the sea, swimming to the boat, brought a man clinging to a timber with him, and climbed into it and ordered the rope to be cut, thus drifting away from the dangers of the oversubscription and the beginnings of long hours in the same boat in the resilience of his rescue operation.

Looking back they would see that the Ocean Monarch was now no longer a proud sailing ship but a floating bonfire on board of which, and in their haste and panic, the passengers could no longer continue to bring up their boxes from below and sort out their money and valuables, spilling much of it in the confusion and losing it forever, in the rush, the desperate fight for space and the chaos.

Orders for action or advice could not be distinguished from screams and shouts of fear and panic lost in a homogenous mass of noise.

The flames continued to increase and move forever forwards, the line of men with buckets had long since stopped in their attempt to put out what was considered to be the seat of the fire as it was having no effect. It was then every person for themselves. For those who had no option to stay on board until there might be chance of rescue, they could only despair that the only serviceable boats had already been lowered, the other two of the four on the ship being consumed within the flames to compound the despair and increase those nagging doubts of being rescued. Timbers and anything that might float were thrown overboard in order to assist those who were struggling in the sea. The carpenter, it seems that this was the first carpenter, William James Moore, was one of the last of the crew on board with the captain, chopping up the timbers with an axe and throwing the pieces overboard to serve as floats. Many passengers and crew jumped overboard and sought out one of these pieces of timber to cling on to. Some succeeded some didn't. Some succeeded for a while then succumbed, all the while in the water being struck by heavy floating timbers that were thrown violently about in the heavy swell. It was at this time that the captain and those few around him by now surrounded by flames, had jumped into the sea only when the flames were within a few feet of them and too hot to handle. They were able to cling onto floating timbers until eventually pulled out of the water by one of the small rowing boats from the yacht of Thomas Littledale on his way back from the regatta at Beaumaris.

There are those who claim they witnessed the Captain leaving in a boat early on in the incident, but others who claimed he had stayed until there was nothing else that could possibly be done. His story is that he had tried in vain to keep order amidst the panic and, in giving assistance and direction to the situation, he advised that the topgallant mast should be cut and a large spar from this was to be attached by a rope to the ship and thrown into the sea, and that as many as possible should jump in after it and cling to it till help should arrive. Many followed his instructions and did survive. Jotham Bragdon had assisted in this, releasing the crotchet brace which supported one of the spars before he too was obliged to leave the ship. When Captain Murdoch had jumped and reached the floating spar, he found that there were too many clinging on to it so he had swum to another piece of floating timber on which he supported himself for a very long hour before being picked up by the boat despatched from the yacht, Queen of the Ocean, which had now arrived on the scene, and was taken there.

William Roberts a man 'before the mast', and one of the thirty four seamen ('and one boy') aboard the Ocean Monarch, was an experienced seaman and was also one of the crewmen in the boat with Jotham Bragdon after he had cut it free for safety's sake, at first bailing it out with their boots, and rowing hither and thither to rescue people from the ship or pulling them out of the water to convey them to the safety of the ships that had come to the aid of the stricken vessel. While still on the ship, and all that was left for him to do was to save his own life, he was about to jump over from the swinging boom to reach the boat but it was too full of people and water so he decided not to. However a woman in the throes of desperation or fear, suddenly grabbed him round the neck and they both fell into the sea. While he himself eventually reached the boat, she was unable to and sadly drowned. He stayed in the boat, which was the waist boat about 21 foot (6.4m) long and able to carry about twenty people, and now as there was no longer a boat on board those on board had to jump, wait for rescue or burn to death. William Roberts assisted with the continuing rescue but when he was eventually exhausted ('fagged out' as reported) in the efforts of continually rowing and dragging the dead weights of heavy sodden and confused survivors aboard to deliver them to the larger vessels, a fresh crew was put into the boat from the Dom Afonso, the Brazilian steam frigate which was now at hand, and to where the little boat had delivered some of the rescued. It is not recorded whether he re-joined the crew of the rescue boat after recovering or not as it returned to rescue more survivors.

THE RESCUERS, THE BURNING SHIP, THE SURVIVORS' STORIES AND THE DEAD

Jotham Bragdon, the major player in the unfolding tragedy, when he could no longer stay on deck, and having seen a second boat, the waist boat, in the water and without enough oars, had quickly stripped and jumped into the water and swam to its aid. He had managed to reach it through the choppy seas and took command of it. By now the yacht that had been first seen in the distance, had arrived. It couldn't come too close due to the flames and the swell, but put down one of its small boats instead. Jotham Bragdon in his own boat, couldn't get back to the burning ship so had cut the attaching rope to prevent it being overloaded and potentially sinking by more people desperately seeking its relative safety. He kept his boat to windward where the occupants frantically continued to bail it out with hats, shoes, cloths and bits of timber and, after about four miles or so, they were picked up by a sloop of which he couldn't remember by name at the time, but later learnt that it was the pilot boat the Queen of Chester. He transferred the passengers to this pilot boat and these were later transferred again from this pilot boat which had gained deep notoriety by the time of the inquests, to a fishing smack before arriving back in Liverpool. Then Jotham Bragdon, having procured some oars from the pilot boat, returned with the three crew members, which would have included William Roberts, making their way back to the burning ship, rowing continuously through the choppy seas, picking up five people en route and taking them back to the pilot boat. On their way back again to the ship they were taken in tow by the Prince of Wales steamer which was fast approaching the scene of the tragedy and to which they delivered another survivor whom they had found clinging to a life buoy. The Prince of Wales brought them close enough to the burning ship as to be able to afford assistance to those struggling for their lives in the water.

Once the steamer was as close as it could safely anchor to the burning ship, its own boat with first mate Mr Batty and three men from the ship's company was lowered. Provided with four oars it made the return journey in between the rescue ships as one of the several little boats, picking up as many passengers as they could who were clinging to anything, including their very lives, that might float, around the front of the burning vessel where many were mostly congregated. The Prince of Wales steamer, of the Dublin Steamship Company, had been on its way ultimately to Wexford, with its Captain Denham (Dani, Daney as alternative, interpreted spellings in the various newspaper accounts) and had left the Mersey at 11am on its way to Bangor. This ship had been by the light ship when the burning ship had been first noticed to the northwest. The situation had become evidently more grave as they approached, and it had come across Jotham Bragdon's boat and it was then that it took it in tow before anchoring as near as it was safe to get to the burning vessel and sending down its own rescue boat and crew.

The first people off the ship, and ultimately surviving, after the alarm had been given, had been some of those from the stern of the ship and who had jumped into one of the boats belonging to the ship and lowered over the side. The second boat, having been haphazardly lowered as well as including some of crew and passengers, later included Jotham Bragdon. The first of these boats making its way to Liverpool was picked up later by a fishing smack, the Town of Liverpool which also later took in the contingent of Jotham Bragdon's boat. Had this first of the ship's boats, like that of Jotham Bragdon's, made its way to the Queen of the Ocean to deposit the passengers there then returned to the burning ship, it was claimed that many more lives could have been saved. There were many frightened screaming, desperate folk in the water clinging on to flotsam for dear life who could have been picked out of the water and rescued from a watery grave by a trip back, as Jotham Bragdon's boat had done. But not everyone possesses heroic status either through instinct or opportunity. These first of the survivors appear to be the sixteen that were landed at Seacombe and given hospitality at the hotel of Mr Parry. They returned over the Mersey to Liverpool on the 8 o'clock ferry and on board was a celebrated comedian, a Mr Basil Baker, who had a whip round for the devastated passengers of the Ocean Monarch who had lost everything. £2 4s (£2 20p; £359 approx 2021) was collected. Basil Baker, described in the Era theatre publication as a 'low' comedian, was a popular act in comedy plays along, sometimes, with his daughter and there were reports that he was a passenger on his way to America and had been rescued from the burning ship, such were the wild and eager stories that were going round without corroboration. But he had just happened to be innocently taking the ferry across the Mersey and there would no doubt be a reference, if not a joke, in there somewhere for him in his later comedic repertoire.

When the ferry reached the pier head and the passengers disembarked, there were tearful scenes of repatriation and warm hugging greetings as those from the Queen of the Ocean met those off the ferry. But, as it's natural to love it is also natural to hate and, some months earlier on the docks, two sailors, (described as 'foreigners') had a clandestinely arranged duel with knives at a location on the docks. Both ended up with lacerated faces and arms. One died at the Northern Hospital and the other was expected to die. The men who had acted as seconds at the duel were not located. But that had been conflict in peacetime, the situation of the Ocean Monarch was peacetime in conflict. These first passengers to arrive at Liverpool had been the very lucky ones but while in the process of rescue, all the time there were still people in the sea pleading and hoping for rescue, if conscious, and people on board watching the flames creep inexorably towards them. There were families being split and others watching their children, siblings or parents disappear or drown in front of them, or lost in the dense smoke and flames below decks unable to reach them. Perhaps those first to be rescued felt the guilt of their good luck or their selfishness.

The vessels that arrived to provide help for the beleaguered passengers and crew of the Ocean Monarch in the continuing saga out at sea were several. They appeared at intervals, one after the other, one of the main players being the Brazilian steam frigate, ultimately known as the Dom Afonso (referred to regularly and ubiquitously in the newspapers as the Affonso), which had been built in Liverpool relatively recently and had not yet seen Brazil. Then there was the Queen of the Ocean, a yacht on its way back from the regatta in Beaumaris, and the Prince of Wales steamer, sailing its regular route across the Irish Sea. The New World, travelling alongside the Ocean Monarch on its own way to New York, on seeing the distress of its sister ship, tacked in the direction of the evidently burning ship and making up the distance between the two, lowered its boats as soon as it was safe to anchor as near as it could get. All these vessels and their human contents became inextricably drawn into the event, offering both practical help through bravery, and compassion through being naturally human. Smaller boats from these vessels were put down onto the sea and interacted with each other and the stricken vessel. The swell rose and fell several feet at a time and to those on the surface struggling in the water at one moment at the top of a crest, would be able see a boat and crew in the nearer or further distance to give them hope, and a moment later to disappear from view in a mighty trough when only death, kept away only by the very last instincts of survival was attempting to take them. And for the lucky ones, when a rope or an arm was caught by one in the boat, emotions would be nil, only that aspect of survival relevant, before the relief of being on the rescue boat was paramount and feelings of being alive yet, in their numbness, unable to understand the loss of friends, family and dear children. Then before that moment with the knowledge and acute realisation of loss, the heart would be allowed to break and the tears of loss and regrets would be allowed to flow.

The Queen of the Ocean had arrived in good time for Captain Murdoch. He had left the ship when nothing else could have been done. If he had been at the fore of the ship when all the passengers were, there was little that could be done anyway as there were no boats to lower down. For those who were too frightened to jump overboard they had to hopefully wait and pray for assistance or, eventually, burn to death. It didn't need the authority of a captain to state that. But as the Captain was in the air after his jump from the ship, somewhere between the rail of the ship and the sea below him, maybe he had a fleeting thought of the unthinkable of his professional failure, or perhaps he was more concerned with blaming the lower class of human being as being also of perceived lower intelligence and had started the fire as such, and he was thus blameless as he'd done everything conceivable in his remit to prevent such a catastrophe. Perhaps after landing in the water, and as he himself was clinging for dear life for over an hour onto one of the many pieces of timber which he had ordered to be cut down and thrown into the sea for the assistance of those who had jumped in and not wanting to meet King Neptune just yet anyway, his thoughts might have been negated in the exigent need to survive, turning perhaps to despair and embarrassment as he was picked up by the yacht the Queen of the Ocean which bore down and hove to as near to the wreck as it was possible to get.

The yacht had seen the impressive ship about three miles away and the ship's company was admiring it when it was suddenly seen to tack and turn with its bow to the north as if it might be returning to Liverpool. Then they saw the smoke issuing from the stern of the vessel and the distress jack, the upturned Union flag, hoisted and so, without hesitation, made for the stricken vessel. The nearer they got, the more harrowing detail of the distress could be observed and the cries of anguish could be heard from the packed front of the vessel. Soon there were several vessels near enough to give assistance, the New World, Sea Queen and the Prince of Wales more immediately, and later the Dom Afonso, and rowing boats propelled strenuously by hardened seafarers went out from these to pick up those from the sea. When they got as close to the ship as they could, lines were attached from ship to ship and many people were saved in this way.

The fire was now streaming from many holes in the ship's side. A quantity of gunpowder had reportedly exploded and though it had not seemed to have caused much damage, it increased the fears and anxieties of those still on the ship, since no-one would have known if there was more powder on the ship and which would be likely to go off at any time. These people were now mostly confined to the front of the vessel and, crawling out on the bowsprit, when there was nowhere else to go apart from the sea, one on top of another, they formed a confused and overloaded mass of people. The masts fell one by one, first the rearmost, the mizzen mast where the fire was most furious and eventually the main mast. Some of those on the deck without any idea of what to do and without any direction capable of being given, would have been crushed to death under the masts as they fell.

Two boats, including the larger paddle box boat capable of taking a large number of people were now rowing their way towards the ship from the Dom Afonso, (this name rather than the Affonso referred to in the newspapers has been taken from the internet wreck site referred to in the acknowledgements at the end) a steam frigate, with its military status, more equipped and capable of reacting to, and dealing with these conditions which resembled the conditions of the heat of battle. Most of the desperate passengers probably wouldn't have known of its military status and the greater experience of its ship's company in dealing with dire situations, but clung on to life for as long as possible. Suffice it to say it was a ship and in the mindset of the desperately hopeful, there was a possibility of rescue. Believing in that could keep one alive.

Mr William Jackson a pawnbroker, of Pinstone Street Sheffield, lost his wife and three children. The children were aged between six and two years. William Jackson had been on the deck close to the captain when a steward rushed up informing the captain of a fire on board. The panic had already started and the whole of the ship had become utterly disorganised in a matter of minutes. He ran to his cabin to bring his family to the deck and when they arrived the fire was so severe, there were only two options, to stay and burn to death or jump and risk death by drowning. He took charge of his two sons, Willy and Richard and his wife took charge of the little girl, Elisabeth. In the struggle and the confusion they made their way to the fore part of the ship, pursued by the fire and obstructed by the crowds in front of them, trying to stay together all the while. Ships were in sight and there was hope of being saved but it would take time, and time was not on the side of anyone on the ship. When the fire became too close and too intense and there was nowhere to go to get away from it, they decided to clamber over the bows and hang on to the ropes of the rigging that were fixed there. Mr Jackson went first with the two little boys and hung on for a short while, but before his wife was able to join him, he fell. Shouting from above and amidst the noise of the sea and the screams of despair of the other passengers, Mrs Jackson told him to look after himself first. Whether he followed her advice or whether there was nothing else he could do, he let go of his two 'dear lambs' and lost them both to the sea. He was able to get hold of another rope and hung by it no doubt with a sickness in the pit of his stomach but still with the hope of saving his wife and daughter. Clinging and swinging and constantly washed over by the sea he saw his wife and daughter by the jib boom where, looking safe, he was confident that they would be saved. It was the last time he would see them. After about three hours he was rescued by a boat from the Sea Queen. A rope was thrown to him from one of the little rowing boats and he and an Irish girl near to him were hauled aboard through the sea. The sea was so rough they could not be put aboard the steamship Dom Afonso and so, as he related the story, the Sea Queen continued its journey to New York. It was a rough passage of thirty five days, twice as long as that expected in the Ocean Monarch and in a derelict emotional state when he wanted to die and throw himself into the sea with no idea whether his wife and daughter had survived, he was treated well and looked after by the captain and a compassionate family from Leeds called Netherwood, who had no doubt tried to convince him that he would indeed meet up with his family in America. When he reached New York, he somehow made his way to Boston to collect the return of the passage money. Here, it was some time before he learnt that his wife and daughter had not survived. Perhaps they had fallen when the foremast collapsed and caused the jib boom to fall into the sea. There is no other report of a New York bound Sea Queen at the scene during the rescue and his story only comes out much later. In a letter to friends he hoped to find work in Boston and if not, then he would return to England the following year. His wife and daughter Elisabeth hadn't lasted very long from the last time he saw them. Little Elisabeth's body was caught in a fisherman's net, hauled aboard and eventually buried at Hoylake on the Wirral peninsula. On the 11th of September Mrs Esther Jackson's body was picked out of the water at the mouth of the river Mersey by the Rhyl packet steamer the Vale of Clywd. At the time the body was identified, her annihilated family was still missing. It was not known for some time that her husband had survived. She was buried at Liverpool attended to by friends and family from Sheffield. The fishing smack Robert had picked up the body of four year old Willy from the sea on 7th September and he was buried at Llandysillio according to the newspaper article. The body of nineteen month old Richard was never recovered or, at least not identified if ever recovered. We don't find out what happened, nor do we find out the name of the Irish girl rescued with Mr Jackson.

One man on board had lost his wife and child and £800 (£64,809.01p). A man named Thompson, a seaman from Liverpool, had jumped into the sea along with his wife and with his child tied to him. He had clung on to his wife as they held on as tightly as possible to the anchor chain as they were constantly buffeted by the sea. After at least an hour, the young child died and, soon after, his wife was swept away. He himself survived. He might have been the Charles Thompson who identified the body of his wife which was picked up by a schooner some days later. He claims at this time that another female came down the rope too soon after them and she caused them to become separated. Perhaps to him these are the same person as, in a confused state, he may have been looking for an excuse for a perceived guilt of losing his wife.

There were plenty of desperate folk clinging to the rigging but eventually the physical strength of some of those left them and they fell into the choppy, cold waters with little chance of staying afloat to survive. The psychological strength, or the frozen fear, of others which forced them to stay on board would be their salvation as much as the 'do or die' leap of faith into the water to reach a piece of floating timber saved others. For many the deepest water they would have had experienced before this day was that in a tin bath or a dip in a pond or a stream in a youthful lark. Sea bathing was becoming popular and trips to the coastal resorts were being made available with cheap railway tickets. For some of those visiting the coast, even a dip in the sea was a fearful excitement and even today is a danger often resulting in tragedy. Skinny dipping or, in the language of the day, 'promiscuous bathing' was conducted at the water's edge, and often from the safety of a bathing van, not in the depths of the ocean and miles from the safety of the shore. In this situation you couldn't paddle ashore through the weight of the waves against your legs since the feet could never reach the security of the bottom to give the body some purchase. Parents watched children drown and children watched their parents drown. Others hoping for survival in the water, clung on to a lifeless body for a float. When that old seafarer was wrecked off Capetown in 1799, he wrote of men of usual coarse, macho behaviour resorting to the supplicant, pleading to their Christian God for mercy and forgiveness, not wanting the gates of Hell to be opened to them should they not reach the shore, where they could plead to be absolved from their sins, while they were subject to the violent, stormy seas that had wrecked the ship as they clung desperately to floating timbers and anything they could get hold of. Apart from the impressed men, usually duped or forced into naval service, these were experienced men, most of who had been a long time at sea. There were those passengers on the Ocean Monarch who had not seen the sea before the last day or two and perhaps ironically had only heard of its promoted health giving properties as administered beneath a relatively warm sun.

Edward James who was saved, lost his wife and £60's (£4,860.68p) worth of savings, John Bell, his wife and £30's (£2,430.34p) worth. Mrs Sale lost her husband, her only child Sarah and her brother. Jane and Elisabeth Murphy of Killarney, John and Mary Warburton, George and Theodosia Jones from Bilston and Andrew Oulton from Dublin were saved.

A bag was seen floating in the sea with the name James K Fellowes printed on it and the correspondent of the newspaper wondered if the bag ever reached its owner, picked out of the sea by another hand and eventually finding its way back to his hands.

It's not known whether James K Fellowes ever saw his bag again but he was a materially privileged man and would not have rued much the loss of any sundry items that it might have contained unless of any sentimental value. He was a watchmaker and jeweller, a profession he had inherited from his father and he had travelled widely from his home town of Lowell, Massachusetts which at six thousand inhabitants was as big as Chicago at the time. He was one of the original members of the Massachusetts state legislature, and had been a member there since its beginnings in 1837 at twenty five years of age. A respected member of the community, he had survived the Ocean Monarch and had a long and successful life ahead of him. He wasn't afraid to travel again across the Atlantic as he visited the Great Exhibition at Crystal Palace in London in 1851. He seems to have been a democrat by political persuasion and bought an estate for $30,000 ($982,829.11) which he donated to the Lowell community to be used as a hospital. Being a cabin passenger he was up on deck before those of the lower decks and was in one of the first boats to be rescued. He might have been seen to throw his bag overboard and follow it, or perhaps he jumped with it but lost it in the process of reaching the safety of the boat. But his fortune was to survive unlike others who did not have that fortune, or others who survived but lost not only all their possessions, but their futures and their loved ones and neither of which could ever be retrieved. James died in 1906 and left a son and three daughters.

Those who had sufficient strength to cling to the rigging in the first place found themselves with no option but to jump as the flames licked up eagerly around them to consume anything that could be put to its torch of fire and the molten lead and pitch dripped onto them. Twenty five year old Mary Ann Taylor of No 1 Victoria Place Leeds was one such person. She was going to join her husband, James, in America who was an overseer of power looms and she had been feeling sea sick and gone to lay down on her bed but, on hearing the news of the fire, she went up on deck to investigate and, on finding the panic there, she quickly returned to her two young children, Sarah, four years and Geoffrey two. She brought them up on deck through, by now, in the ever increasing smoke, nearly suffocating in the process. But the searing heat of the deck became too much for the feet to bear and, in desperation, she found a handkerchief and tied the children to her she as much as she practically could. She then lowered herself and her children over the side by a rope and then grabbed onto the rigging fixed to the side of the ship on which there were many others clinging on for life. It was a desperate effort to hold with one arm her children and manoeuvre across the ropes and hold on with the other. The sea was choppy and the waves continually soaked all who were in her situation and this constant soaking eventually suffocated the children making them so much heavier for her weakening physical strength. Then out of compassion an Irishman cut the dead children loose and they fell into the water. Mary survived to tell her story but she had a long life to get through with the experience of losing two of her children in this manner. The sympathetic Irish hand, was one whose owner was perhaps inured to the sight of death as he lived through the famine which was most severe in his home country, and which had prejudice favourably only of privilege, not of age, politics or religion. Before this journey perhaps he had previously seen his children die of starvation before his very eyes.

Joshua Wilson, a letter press printer from Strangeways, Manchester, and who was later to bitterly condemn all and sundry on the ship, was lowering his wife who was clutching their child which was tied to her, down to one of the first rescue boats but she lost her grip from the wet and swinging rope and, fell into the sea. It's not certain who eventually jumped first as reports differ but he was momentarily reunited with his wife and child in the water. She was hanging on to his neck until a strong surge of the water loosened her grip and both she and the child went under its cruel surface and he never saw them again.

On the relieved side of human experience, the Nottingham Review was pleased to publish a letter from three young men, John Freckleton, a single man and tailor, and Elisha Bannister, this latter a shoemaker who had left his wife and two children behind in order to seek work in America, and James Walker, single and a warehouse clerk who had been unemployed for a year and who also wanted to try his luck in America. They had all left the town and had survived the disaster, being helped aboard the Dom Afonso. They had been aboard the Ocean Monarch while it was at the dockside for four days before sailing and having been fortunate enough to have been rescued, were landed at Liverpool about 10pm on the day. They had been taken to the police station for clothing and there they met with a Mr Roughton of the Steampacket Inn who gave them good accommodation at his establishment. Back to the agony of human experience, it was understood, but not ascertained by the newspaper that a woman and five of her children from the town had perished, leaving only her eldest daughter a survivor, though an uncle of hers was reported to be a survivor. A young Irish lad, Daniel O'Leary had rescued his sister by pulling her out of the water by her hair as she was helplessly sinking. They both survived having been picked up by one of the small boats and put aboard the Dom Afonso.

As time wore on during the incident, the anchored ship became aflame almost along its full length and the scores of remaining passengers had packed the forward part of the ship even more densely. With the mizzen mast already gone, it was the turn of the main mast to succumb to the destructive hunger of the flames and crashed down in view of the second ship to arrive. By means of an attached rope from ship to ship, the small boats with their determined crews continued to pull people out of the water and ferry many of them across to the waiting safety of the larger vessels.

Bodies and flotsam littered the surface of the waves accompanied in the air above them by the screams of those in peril and the fearful noise of the animals which had no chance of rescue at all and were left to their fate.

In the beginning, Mr H Powell of Portman place, Maida Hill, London escaped with his life, whether by divine providence or his own conscious decision. He at first went forward out of his cabin to where everyone was crowded into the only conceivable concept of safety there, limited as it was. There was a great consternation as to why none of the boats had been lowered and Mr H Powell thought it a good idea to move away from the crowd on the forecastle and stand close to the edge there so he would not be involved in the inevitable panic rush when any of the rescue boats should actually arrive, as the crowds would see a single chance of escape. He made his way to the centre of the vessel which was burning fiercely, but it was his good fortune to arrive at the moment when some of the crew had just thrown the boat overboard and were jumping into the water. The flames were almost on him. There was no time for procrastination. A decision had to be made immediately. He took off his overcoat and caught hold of the rope that attached the boat to the ship but once reaching the end of it, immediately sank into the water and lost his grip. He surfaced and when an Irishman, in desperation pleaded with him to hold onto him, his weight sent them under again but this second man lost his grip and Mr H Powell was able to catch hold of the rope again. He heard the mate shout out to cut the ropes to cast the boat adrift. And after it had been done he found himself on the wrong bit of rope but then he managed to grab hold of someone's legs who was clinging to the side of the boat. With an effort he was able to climb over his man and drop himself into the boat. The little boat was crowded and the sea was choppy. The mate was able to organise things a little and with three crew men, there was some sense of order. The danger however was nowhere near over but fortunately this turned out to be the boat that Jotham Bragdon had commandeered and all aboard bailed the boat out with whatever came to hand, boots, caps and bits of timber. At first the little boat was never very far away from the burning vessel and in earshot of the cries, pleas and screams of the desperate people on board. They saw the masts fall one by one and heard the explosion of the powder. Eventually they were transferred to the Welsh Pilot boat from which they were then transferred to the fishing smack, whose owner, William Syers would have seen it all before during his time under the mast with Lord Nelson in the French wars. Mr H Powell arrived at Seacombe, today the terminus of the ferry across the Mersey from Liverpool, 'about seven o'clock in the evening, after seven hours' exposure, without shoes or stockings, hat or shirt to my back.'

There was quite a swell in the sea which was littered with many passengers who had seen no way out but to jump off, one woman reportedly cutting her throat rather than suffer the fear of drowning. Others clung to flotsam, frantically thrown into the water from the ship for their use. Others did not surface again once they had jumped in, mothers losing children and children surviving when their parents couldn't. Mr and Mrs Dow from Glasgow were in the water for two hours before being rescued, all the while being tossed and buffeted against the side of the ship, clinging for all their lives were worth onto a spar with a mixture of despair and hope, the fear of drowning more than the determination to live keeping them alive. They could count themselves lucky. More women than men were lost and the reason given that women were less able to look after themselves than the men, not that perhaps the dress tradition of the female was less conducive to climbing down the ropes or rigging or for surviving in the water when they reached it. Lycra sportswear or yoga pants are only the privilege of the greater relative freedom of the modern woman in which, on occasion, seemingly, the evidence of excess bottomry is revealed in desperation to be set free from the bursting limits of critically uncomfortable confinement. Wives lost husbands and husbands lost wives. Both lost children. Children became separated and lost their parents. When lives were saved, everything connected to it was more than likely lost, money and goods and even the clothes which were sometimes dispensed with in the mighty effort to keep afloat in the great mass of the unforgiving ocean. The Captain's order at the beginning that any movable and floating object to be thrown overboard to assist those many that had jumped from the ship in their panic had saved many people including himself. His plea for order and calm went unheard or unheeded in the panic of survival. At that point in the beginnings, a small vessel could be seen approaching. All would survive if only order could be kept. There are more ships on the way. The two boats that were almost immediately dropped over the side by crew and passengers alike were in danger of sinking with their unpreparedness or their excessive payloads. The fire grew fiercer and had control of the aft and the mid part of the ship. It was eating its way up the masts. At this point before a single person had evacuated the ship, it had become evident that these would soon collapse.

The New World was another of the ships that were to play a significant part in the rescue but we don't learn of its full role until the papers report its story on its return in December of the same year, its heroics ignored while the evidence of others was praised. Captain Knight was proceeding to New York with over seven hundred migrants on board his ship. He had discharged the pilot by the Bell Buoy at 8am, about the same time as the Ocean Monarch had discharged its own pilot. The wind was generally northwest and all was going well as he took his glass and observed the other vessels around him which included the Ocean Monarch, Sea Queen and the Ocean Queen yacht. As his glass swept the ocean he noticed that the

Ocean Monarch appeared to be on fire as smoke was curling up from it in alarming quantities.

It was claimed, through insufficient evidence and false reporting, that the captain of this sister ship of the Ocean Monarch, the New World was reluctant to take part in any rescue attempt and would have preferred to travel on and leave the Ocean Monarch to its fate knowing that there would be other ships around to do the rescuing, and it was also claimed that it was only the chastising pleas of the crew that turned the Captain's sentiment to the rescue of the other ship. The New World however, had stayed where it was and the boats were put out. But whatever the specifics of the truth, which would more credit its captain's humanity and his captaincy, rather than defile it, he immediately took measures to take his ship the six miles towards the burning vessel and lowered his cutter and lifeboat with instructions to the men to be careful, but not to return until everyone was off the burning ship. Furnished with ropes, boat hooks and spare oars, the men set off towards the stricken vessel. Other assistance was already there but, as the fire progressed the boats could not get safely close to the ship because of the falling, burning timbers, rope stays, chain cables and rigging. It was easier, despite the heavy swell, to pick out those who had fallen or jumped into the water, those that were alive, anyway.

The yacht, the Queen of the Ocean, being the nearest and the first of the rescue boats to arrive, had consequently been the first to take passengers off the ship, eventually thirty two in all, including Captain Murdoch. It had a large capacity boat at its disposal. It would be over an hour before the frigate, Dom Afonso would arrive with its greater capabilities. From close at hand, parents could be made out with their children tied to themselves with whatever suitable material was to hand, even making ropes of handkerchiefs, longer than the standard sizes of today of course, and climbed out onto the rigging and clinging there out on the side of the ship, constantly battered by the choppy seas which reached up to them from below as the flames reached down to them from above. Occasionally they could be seen from the decks of the recue ships falling into the sea as strength deserted them.

The boats eventually arrived, one by one again and again slowly making their way through the choppy seas and through the dead bodies floating by uncannily macabre just a little way under the surface. Occasionally a body would have life in it and it was hauled aboard. Taken back to the larger ships these were the lucky ones. The frigate, Dom Afonso approached and settled itself as near as it could safely get to the stricken vessel. A boat was sent out and warped the frigate to the stricken vessel and along this lifeline the boat made its way there and back again and again, and in this way had rescued over a hundred people.

The steamer Prince of Wales was on its way to Bangor and had left Liverpool and diverted to the scene of the fire and took in the twenty passengers it had collected from the boats before continuing its journey to Bangor and delivering its survivors into the generosity of the shore dwellers there. Along with the New World packet ship, on its way to New York, the Queen of the Ocean yacht on its way back from Bangor, all had come to help, giving assistance by sending boats down and across to the flames and together they again saved numerous lives before the Dom Afonso had arrived.

A passenger describes the incident from the deck of the steam ship, Prince of Wales. He was admiring the beauty of the Welsh coast with his telescope and, when he turned it seawards, he saw the smoke from a ship which he took to be the smoke from a coal fired steamer beyond it. It was about four miles away and, with a little more curiosity, he studied it further and noticed that it was a ship on fire and informed the captain, Denham, who immediately turned his vessel towards it. As they drew nearer, closer to the burning ship itself, the extent of the tragedy began to unfold. First a man clinging to a buoy was pulled out of the water about two miles away from the burning ship and then they came across increasing amounts of floating material, cabbages he notices specifically as if a crate had been broke open to distribute them into the sea, but the harrowing truth became evident when lifeless bodies in numbers were seen floating just beneath the surface.

They could see many people crowded onto the front of the vessel and those clinging to the rigging fixed to the ship's side were being constantly submerged as the swell of the ocean lifted the vessel up and down through ten to twelve feet of constant surge. One moment they were lifted out of the water and at another they were thrown beneath it, some with children tied to their own bodies. This swell drowned the young children before it suffocated the adults. As they anchored as near as they could possibly get, other ships were already offering their assistance, and now the pitiable cries and screams for mercy and the crackling and fire-spitting noise and, among the screams and desperately supplicant prayers of the passengers was the noise of the cow and the frightened bleating of the sheep neither of which could be afforded any kind of rescue, and could be clearly heard. It didn't matter that the human cries were the 'cries of the lowest class of Irish and the manufacturing districts of Lancashire' (and both of which groups were forced to use violence against the class system, when requests and demands for basic human rights were not being considered). They were human beings and would claim that right. It would take acts of bravery and selflessness to rescue many and further acts of extreme bravery and selflessness to rescue others.

Soon they picked up the boat from the burning ship with Jotham Bragdon and three crew members on board while it was on its way back to the Ocean Monarch after it had delivered its human cargo to the Welsh pilot boat. It took the little boat in tow towards the stricken vessel ahead of them. On arrival at the Ocean Monarch there were scenes of utter chaos. Ships were already there and gallant efforts were being made to rescue the remaining passengers. Once at the ship Jotham Bragdon took his boat to the bows, manoeuvring through the dead bodies and was able to rescue three people from that part. Soon after that he pulled a woman and child from the sea but the child died as soon as it reached the safety of the boat, to leave a mother to engage with the extremes of human loss and despair. The boat from the Prince of Wales refurnished him with more oars. He managed to get the boat to the bows of the ship once more and tried to persuade the people there to jump, but most were too scared only two, a man and a woman took the leap for life and he was able to rescue them, taking them this time to the Dom Afonso which would have been the nearest and most sensible option of the moment.

By the time the Dom Afonso and the steamship Prince of Wales had both arrived, the men of the New World had been at their task for over an hour, showing disciplined obedience to the officers who were with them, soaked to the skin and refusing any stimulating, alcoholic drink, that was the macho adrenalin producing juice of courage. They drank only the water that was offered to them on their return to a vessel on which they could despatch their boatloads of survivors before returning to pick up more. There was about an hour where it was thought that the ship was sinking and it was too dangerous to continue and the 'poor creatures' still on the ship had lost all sense of reason and sense to save themselves and would have to be tragically and agonisingly left to their fate. There were still people at the forefront of the vessel over an hour after the fire had started. One woman was there because another woman had pushed her out of the way to get the last rope down the side of the ship to the waiting boat. She awaited her fate expecting to die. Another old man was there with a child clinging to him. Its mother had drowned and the child, a girl was on her own. She clung to the old man for security. He knew that neither of them could survive in the sea. He wasn't going to desert her dependence upon him and probably praying for rescue was his only option. But it wasn't God who saved him, along with all the remaining passengers of the ship, but the selfless bravery of another human being and his companions. Whatever the slight variations in detail of the stories, it was a single human being who scaled the heights up the ropes from a boat in the choppy seas to rescue the last surviving passengers on board. But the finale of the rescue didn't take place until relatively favourable conditions did return, when the New World's lifeboat dashed under the bowsprit once more when Frederick Jerome, the most renowned and lauded of the rescuers, was ordered to shin up the rope that had been the top mast stay and let down the remaining few passengers one by one.

Back to the beginning of the event, the first vessel at the scene had been the Queen of the Ocean, a yacht owned by Thomas Littledale, (T and H Littledale and Co Brokers) of Liverpool and sailed by a Liverpool crew. Resident at Highfield House, Old Swan, and owning three warehouses and the Counting House in the Exchange Buildings, he was Commodore of the Royal Mersey Yacht Club and with him, along with the crew, were Thomas Hesketh, Mr Tobin, Mr Falk and Mr Anfrere as well as Sir Thomas Hesketh, High Sheriff of Rufford Hall and his chaplain, who were out for a sail with their friend.

This Day, (Thursday) the 12th instant,
at the Brokers' office, 13, Exchange-buildings,
3329 Bags Bengal RICE,
390 Bales fine JUTE,
just arrived per Mary Somerville: east side Prince's Dock.
Apply to Messrs. TAYLOR, POTTER and Co. Merchants, or to
T. and H. LITTLEDALE and Co. Brokers.

This Day, (Thursday) the 12th instant, at one o'clock,
60 Tons Saldanah Bay GUANO,
ex Hope.—Apply to Messrs. BOLDS and Co. Merchants, or to
T. and H. LITTLEDALE and Co. Brokers.

This Day, (Thursday) the 12th instant, at one o'clock,
at the Brokers' office, 13, Exchange-buildings,
30 Tons Patagonia } GUANO.
30 Tons Saldanha Bay }
Apply to T. and H. LITTLEDALE and Co. Brokers.

Gore's Liverpool General Advertiser 12th October 1848

Captain Thomas Littledale was on his way back from Beaumaris where he had attended the regatta there and as they passed at some distance they admired the stately ship that was positioned a few miles east of the Great Orme Head. All of a sudden, it seemed that it was manoeuvring in order to turn back to Liverpool and at the same time they noticed the flag of distress raised as flames suddenly burst out of the stern of the vessel. Mr Littledale and friends immediately made for the ship in distress and approached as near as possible. The scene that they witnessed before them of flames 'bursting with immense fury', of the piercing and heart rending shrieks and pleas for help of men, women and children facing imminent death to two of the greatest fears, burning and drowning, inspired those with nerve to match their compassion for humanity, to risk a life to save life. Those on the deck of the burning ship who couldn't make it to the fore part of the vessel to escape the flames, threw themselves into the water. The masts, consumed by the flames fell down one by one as the boat went out from the Queen of the Ocean with the hardy few and capable oarsmen, leaving those on board to watch helplessly.

When the yacht had arrived at the scene, the ship was aflame from stern to mid and the forward part of the vessel was packed with frightened people screaming in their despair for any kind of assistance that could be given. The smoke had quickly become so intense that very soon after the start of the fire, William Walker of the crew had no longer been able to hold the wheel. Samuel Moody another crew member had jumped overboard when the fire appeared to be out of control and was saved by the boat which Mr Littledale's yacht had just put out. Men and women, sometimes with their children in their arms were jumping off the burning ship in a vain attempt at self-preservation, but many sank beneath the water never to rise again. Such a situation would awaken the hero potential in any compassionate human being and in this way, in Mr Littledale, a man of the sea, it was consequently awoken. In all, by his exertions, he had manged to save thirty two lives, including that of the Captain Murdoch. As he ordered his boat to be lowered he witnessed the mizzenmast, the rearmost mast collapse into the fire and, shortly after, the main mast followed. Those clinging to the side of the ship were burnt badly by both the molten pitch and lead oozing out of the joints all along the sides and which the heat of the fire had liquefied. In this way some of those who clung to the sides of the ships lost their grip as the fire burnt through their hands. Many of those corpses subsequently retrieved and many of the survivors had scorched hands and burn marks to the body.

The crowded foremost part of the ship became even more crowded and even noisier. Many clambered onto the jib, the furthermost position from the fire, and there were so many people on it, sometimes one on top of another, that when the foremast collapsed and went overboard, the jib boom became unsecured and the whole fell into the water. Some managed to regain the ship, others floated away on spars which had been thrown overboard to assist those already in the water and others unable to do either, succumbed to the power of the seas and drowned. Many of these people would have never seen the sea before and be ignorant of its dangers, until challenged by it to face life or death while within its grasp, the alleged smoker or fire raiser in the hold among them. Many in the innocence of their ignorance were drowned in such a way. To find oneself immersed in the cold sea with a stiff wind blowing creating a heavy swell when you had no knowledge of the sea or the power of its waters meant that most would have to hope for rescue by others than be able to save themselves by their own means.

Those observers on the larger ships watched quite helplessly as the passengers of the stricken ship tried to save themselves or resigned themselves to a death at the extremes of natural fears and dread. Some they could see jump into the water. Some they could see staying, fearful of jumping, ironically frozen to the spot in the intense heat of the prolonged moment. Those in the sea hampered the rescue of those still on board because the small boats could not at first reach the burning ship. Only the small boats could get anywhere near. The larger vessels had to anchor further off. One lifeless body of a young woman was caught in the rigging and the corpse was constantly dashed against the body of the ship by the waves as the onlookers watched helplessly from the safety and security of the own vessels. Hardly able to help the living or partly living, there was no way that anything could be done for the dead, unnatural that it seemed to the ordinary human being. A young Irish girl was amongst the survivors. She had no parents with her, presumably lost or drowned and she could only speak Gaelic and could only give her name as Kate. It would be a while before a passenger who could converse with her in her own language could offer any verbal comfort or indeed any explanation or justification of being human and the life she had been given and was expected to get through before her. And they were able to observe the courage of the sailor from the New World, later to be identified and lauded as Frederick Jerome as he single-handedly rescued those last remaining passengers on the bow of the ship. And, in the words of a 'gentleman' on board the Prince of Wales while observing those still on board, 'A beautiful characteristic feature of disinterested human kindness was shown by an old man, Samuel Fielding,' a fustian weaver from Glossop, about sixty years of age. He sat on the edge of one of the sides of the head beneath the bowsprit, holding in his arms a beautiful child, from two to three years old. The old man says it clung to him after its mother sunk and he took it in his arms till he and it were saved, the last two persons off the boat by the unselfish bravery of Frederick Jerome, whose hands were burnt with his tight grip on the chains which became hotter and hotter as the heat increased. Another account gives the child in the arms of a woman, not a man, such was the natural confusion of events and is the one depicted on the medal of the Humane Society, struck for the occasion. Another of the last few survivors was a young girl from Rochdale who earlier on had been the last of her female family to drop down by a rope, each in turn but just as it was her turn, another adult woman, gripped by the selfish need to survive before anyone else, grabbed the rope from her and let herself down. All the women who went before her lost their lives and the young woman resigned herself to her fate on the burning ship, a fate that would see her rescued from the resignation of death by the brave seaman Jerome. Another woman having been pushed overboard by a helping hand when she was too scared to jump herself found herself in the death grasp of another woman who had been badly bruised and her head shattered and crushed in the time she had been in the water and hardly alive herself. This woman didn't last very long, her head collapsed as she died but her body reportedly provided a float which was clung to by the other woman until she found herself rescued and taken on board the Dom Afonso. Another woman who had braved the jump to get hold of a rope, though succeeding in grasping the rope, was caught in the heavy swell and, bashed by the heavy floating timbers, her body became entangled in the rigging on the side of the vessel. Hers was the lifeless body that hung there washed and swung by the heavy swell in full view of the helpless onlookers.

Admiral Grenfell was on the Brazilian steam frigate Dom Afonso, and a ship recently built at Liverpool for the Brazilian navy and the vessel was out for a trial run to Dublin. For its own sake mechanically, and for all those who it was able to rescue, it was fortunately a very uneventful trial, for at the end of September it had to be taken into dock for repair to mechanical failures developed as it was passing the Skerries off Ireland on its way to Lisbon and then home to Rio de Janeiro and consequently had to return to Holyhead. From there it was, ignominiously perhaps, towed by a Holyhead steamer to Liverpool where it could be docked for the necessary repairs to be carried out. All the dispatches it was carrying would now be well out of date and the proud manufacturers of its steam engine and paddles, Messrs Benjamin Hick and Son of Bolton, no doubt somewhat alarmed.

It had arrived on the scene about an hour and a half after the Queen of the Ocean, having to make eight knots speed against the wind and eventually arrived into the thick of the action.

It would have been seen in the distance by those desperately clinging on to life. On board the Dom Afonso was the one armed Englishman, John Pascoe Grenfell a man who had achieved the position of Admiral of the Brazilian navy and who was eventually rewarded for his part in the rescue. He had seen much action in South America where he had lost his right arm in a naval engagement fighting against the Argentinians in 1826. It was not in the mindset of a Victorian gentleman and soldier to witness the women, perceived as the 'weaker sex', and children as collateral damage to conflict and he was foremost in providing as much assistance as he was able to. Admiral Grenfell was resident in Liverpool at the time as Brazilian consul-general and the frigate was out in its trial run on a leisurely cruise before it had come across the Ocean Monarch.

The Dom Afonso was a military ship and thus much more prepared and trained for difficult situations than a civilian ship. It had on board two paddle box boats and four standard boats. The ship didn't have a full complement of crew since it was only on a trial run and there were not sufficient hands to man all the boats. But the paddle box was lowered in seconds and the one-armed Admiral Grenfell was not averse to jumping into it. On reaching the burning ship, a hawser was eventually successfully attached to it and the boats were able to bring many people by this method across the choppy seas to the safety of the frigate. Most were in the water, generally women perceived as universally helpless and children (actually everybody was virtually helpless but more women appeared to have the children with them). By now all the masts had gone from the Ocean Monarch and fire was pouring out from holes in the side. There were about a hundred people packed into the front of the ship and the jib boom had been crammed with those clinging on to life. Those on the Dom Afonso witnessed the collapse of the foremast, taking away with it the support for the jib and which also fell into the sea with all those clinging on to it. Some drowned, some clung to floating spars and others made it back to the side of ship.

The Dom Afonso was commanded by the Marquis da Lisboa and, of no lesser social privilege and esteem, were the Duke and Duchess of Aumale, recently exiled from France, the Brazilian Consul Joao Francisco Froes, the Prince de Joinville, claimant to the French throne and married to the daughter of the Brazilian Emperor Pedro, the daughters of Admiral Grenfell and other 'distinguished individuals'. The party had stayed for a while in Liverpool at the Railway Hotel, Lime Street, owned by a Mr Birchenough.

The Brazilian Government was keen to give concessions to European emigrants. Perhaps these emigrants on the Ocean Monarch would have been better off going there. While this would have helped those few who were able to buy land and develop it, it wouldn't have helped the great majority of crew and passengers who made up the ship's contingent who were generally without sufficient funds to buy up land. Distinguished as the ship's company was in social definition, there was no lack of assistance and compassion shown in saving the lives of fellow human beings as real and naked as they were at bath time in the eyes of their Christian maker. The pitiable cries and screams and pleas for help amid the chaos of the burning ship must have stirred even the most unmovable of consciences and melted hearts as deeply frozen as permafrost.

The Dom Afonso had anchored to the windward and immediately sent out a rope to attach to the burning ship. In this way the boats that were put down could manoeuvre to and fro between the vessels with greater ease. Ann Roper, in contradiction to the general perception of her belonging to the 'weaker sex', tied herself and her child to a rope and jumped off the side of the ship, clinging on for dear life until the two somehow became separated in the sea. Ann was rescued by a boat and taken to the Dom Afonso and eventually reached the Northern Hospital suffering from badly bruised legs. Mrs Grenfell took personal charge of a young child who was barely alive for whom no parent could be found and who was subject to nightmares in its sleep. On arriving back at Liverpool it was taken to the Northern Hospital where it presented a sublime moment of human experience, reported modestly as a 'deeply affectionate moment', when it was reunited as the same Mary Roper was found to be its mother. Perhaps it slept well that night in the clinging mother's arms and both would have awoken to a blissful morrow.

The military training, experience and precision of the Admiral on board came in to play. When the available boats were lowered, Admiral Grenfell jumped into one and the Marquis de Lisboa another. The relatively new invention, the paddle box boat, capable of holding up to a hundred armed troops and baggage had been launched. It was dropped into the water and floated like a cork. Capable of performing well in heavy seas, it was being argued as a necessity for any vessel of a certain capacity to carry in case of emergencies. As a naval frigate, the Dom Afonso carried one. In all these methods and the efforts of those involved saved many, many lives as the frightened and forever grateful and lucky passengers saved from death but not from a life of great loss and psychological pain treatable not by the science of psychotherapy but only by the compassion of others when this could be expressed and is equally effective. There were 160 of these people from the Dom Afonso and 140, including 23 crew members were landed at Liverpool, the remaining 20 preferring to stay on the ship, presumably because they had lost everything and were fearful of the nothingness of their annihilated hopes and dreams that would greet them once back on land, or were too ill to be moved immediately. A steamer had reportedly docked alongside the Dom Afonso and the frigate took three surgeons on board, there being many casualties with broken limbs. Every assistance and comfort was afforded the rescued survivors on board the naval frigate.

Twenty four year old Mrs Mary Sale was eventually landed from this ship. She had lost her husband James, her brother and only child a daughter, Sarah and she was exceedingly bruised. Children, confused and in shock and bereaved of parents could only voice their names and give some information on their siblings' names. The Vice Consul and all the ships' passengers, supplied those on board with clothing as much as possible. Many had broken limbs when they were brought ashore. The bodies of those that had died, once landed, were placed in the 'dead-house' at the end of the dock.

One of these was a dead baby. Perhaps the mother could not bear to leave it while on board the rescue vessel or perhaps it was alone and had not been identified and if it had lived might not have had any parents to be re-united with. There was no mention of the Duke d'Aumale. Perhaps he perceived those in dire need of assistance as belonging to the Third Estate of the French Revolution which had slaughtered his parents and aristocratic ancestors and he was 'nothing but a powerless spectator of the most deplorable catastrophes.' This did not concern the Prince de Joinville (of the same royal family and who had brought the remains of Napoleon from St Helena to France), for he stripped off his fine clothes to his waist and was indefatigable in assisting the rescued passengers off the small boats and up on to the frigate. Acting as caterer to the party aboard the Dom Afonso was Mr Lynn, of the Waterloo Hotel in Liverpool and who was always around when there was any catering to be done especially for big events, and once on shore he generously opened his doors for the assistance of the survivors.

THE LAST ONES OFF

The finale to the rescue took place at the bow of the ship where all those who couldn't or wouldn't clamber down or make a leap of faith down into the water to be collected by the boats, had gathered. All the while the personnel on the two steamers were deliberating how to rescue these remaining people stranded there. They thought the bow of the ship could be climbed up by the ropes but a theory is often too severe for the practice. Burning ropes and scorching chains hung down and swung sometimes quite violently to and fro making the scaling of them unimaginably difficult even for the spiderlike skills of a seasoned seaman. The bowsprit was no longer there. It had collapsed when its support was undermined by the collapse of the foremast. Some of those who had fallen into the water due to its collapse, had been pulled out by the actions of the little boats and the determined and willing hands within them, supplied by the bigger vessels. Those that hadn't survived the result of the collapse were left to float along as macabre corpses just below the surface for, as nothing could be done for them, the living had to be the priority. There had been a lull in the proceedings as the sea conditions, trying to have the last say, prevented the boats from reaching the ship, but as soon as conditions would let them the boats returned, rising and falling quite severely in the swell by the bow of the ship, their crews contemplating on how to rescue the last remaining few who remained stranded between life and death above them on the deck.

The boats below the bow had been back and forth already several times between the stricken ship and the rescue ships, and the personnel had changed within them several times also, as there was an opportunity for an essential rest for exhausted limbs. 1848 belonged to the decade when lifeboats were being located on the shorelines. The one on the Fylde Coast where the body of Alice Wrigley had been washed up had been provided in 1846. By 1851,

J K Fellowes survivor of the tragedy, would have considered with interest the new self-righting lifeboats on show at the Great Exhibition at Crystal Palace when he returned across the Atlantic from his American home to visit. But it was a relatively new idea and shipwreck victims had to rely upon the impromptu actions and bravery of the people of the shoreline if lucky enough to be near a shore, just as the victims of the Ocean Monarch had to rely upon the inventiveness, determination and courage of those around them, who had initially been unaffected by the tragedy.

But, as the boats helplessly bobbed up and down below the ship something had to be done to climb up to the deck in order to effect a rescue of the pathetic figures that looked more like automatons then human beings. For those people adhering to the last hopes of rescue it was the good fortune that the two main players in the rescue were together. Jotham Bragdon and Frederick Jerome were in the same boat. Both were seasoned seafarers and they had sailed together before. Perhaps they'd had a glass of ale with each other at a dockside inn in Liverpool the day before sailing to recount seafarers' tales and perhaps, in the sailors' vernacular on parting, they had wished each good luck on their separate journeys. Jotham, had witnessed the skills and bravery of his former shipmate off New York when their ship the Henry Clay was stranded there a mile and a half off shore, buffeted by the seas and the passengers and crew in the gravest of dangers. At that time Frederick Jerome had jumped off the ship into cold and rough seas and took about two hours to reach the shore (as reported) carrying a lead line attached to the ship over his shoulder. With this, those on the shore were able to attach a carriage, a kind of bosun's chair, later to be called the breeches buoy, and the passengers one by one were taken off the ship and all were saved. The alternative to Frederick's brave swim ashore would have been the rocket fired line from the shore to a ship in distress. It was an age when this equipment was being deployed here and there around the coasts of Britain but the inhabitants of this coast did not have the use of one. Fortunately a man of the calibre of Frederick Jerome had been present at the time.

There is a confused story of how both the two men came to be together on the same boat before the bow of the burning Ocean Monarch. Frederick Jerome was the mate on board the New World, a ship that allegedly in the beginning had turned away from the tragedy, the captain it was wrongly understood, not wanting to delay his journey but to carry on and leave the Ocean Monarch to its fate or its rescue attempts to others, until he was persuaded to put down the boats by the pleas of the crew members. Frederick Jerome was in one of these little boats nevertheless put down into the sea from this ship and intimately involved in the rescue attempts.

Jonathan Bragdon in his several trips alternatively to and from the Prince of Wales and the Dom Afonso had, in his own account, had come across Frederick Jerome, his former shipmate who had been in the paddle box boat of the Dom Afonso while he was transferring two surviving passengers to the Dom Afonso itself. They greeted each other, and it is difficult to believe that they greeted each other in a language other than purely maritime and, in the heaving seas, drenched to the skin and the acute emergency of the situation and adrenalin fully rigged with a stiff following wind that it would not be the language that might be spoken in such a formal occasion as a wedding, a job interview or the somewhat Bowdlerised version of a celluloid Hollywood hero. Both agreed that it would be a good idea for Frederick to join Jonathan's crew. Jonathan because he knew of Frederick's previous courage and suitability of temperament and Frederick because, as the serial lifesaver he was to become, he perhaps wanted to be always in the thick of things, and so a man was exchanged for him.

The problem they now faced together, was how in a practical way to get the remaining people off the front of the damaged ship. When they reached the choppy seas below the front of the burning vessel one version is that Frederick Jerome, in his own decision, thought he would be able to scale the hanging rigging and lower down those last few still hoping for rescue by rope and thus he freely volunteered for it. Another version is that he was ordered or asked to do, which presupposes someone more senior than the two chief mates in the boat. Both Admiral Grenfell and the Prince de Joinville had both been in the boats at one time but, whatever the motive or instruction, he nevertheless completed the task with complete success. Looking above him from the rolling boat which he and the other oarsmen were trying to keep steady it was evident that he would have to clear away any obstacles in the process. With this always a necessary possibility in the back of his mind, Jotham Bragdon had collected some axes and knives from the Afonso on this occasion and so, with a rope around his shoulders, Frederick Jerome, reprising the actions of his former heroics off the coast of America, took off his coat and jumped into the sea, swimming the short but difficult distance to catch hold of a piece of dangling rigging, and scaling this, as the only bit that was not on fire, with the skill of a seasoned sailor. While Jotham Bragdon and crew held the boat, Frederick Jerome gained the deck. It was not an easy task as ropes, rigging and timbers were hanging down to obstruct progress but through determination, acquired skills and physical strength he had reached the top. He had not given up once before while on, or, rather off, the Henry Clay and had rescued the lives of hundreds as he was reportedly, at an extreme, more than two hours in the sea before he had arrived exhausted on the shore. On this second occasion he would reprise the role for the rescue of the remaining few on the Ocean Monarch. Once he had gained the deck, he was able to lower the passengers down one by one which was no mean feat for him and no joy ride for the passengers in avoiding the swinging ropes and scorching cables but to the cheers of their success from those watching from both steamers. The New World with its Captain Knight was nearly a mile away to the north at the time and hadn't witnessed the bravery of the ship's first mate. He is reported as being naked and, as most of the remaining survivors were women, he might have had a little reward by being able to show off, if naked meant naked and not just stripped down to essential underwear to protect his identifying masculinity from the ravages of fire and sea. For their part the women were probably far beyond the realms of frightening experience to indulge in the excitement of being rescued by a naked man. He lowered them one by one while the flames burned fiercely behind them all. Once near the waiting boat, they were hooked by their clothes with a boat hook if they couldn't be reached by the arms, and then pulled into the relative safety of the boat, crying with gratitude or numbed with relief. As each person was hauled aboard in turn, there was a round of cheers and clapping in the boat and in the watching vessels beyond. An old, grey-haired man it is usually understood, though other reports have him as a woman clutching a child, was too afraid or too stubborn to move and he had to be persuaded, with a little physicality and no doubt with a few severe words of unabashed nature from Frederick Jerome to eventually move and save himself and the child, which was alive and scared in his arms. Three louder cheers greeted this person, whether man or woman (as the confused stories report one or the other) and then three even louder ones for Frederick Jerome when he regained the waiting boat, the rescue having been successfully completed. These were the last people from the ship. Other small boats from the several ships giving assistance had previously rescued many and there were cheers of collective relief and triumph but a sadness set aside no doubt for those previously forced to jump by fear or by necessity due to the searing heat and had drowned.

In the confusion of subsequent reports, one states that Frederick Jerome had then reached the boat of the Dom Afonso first rather than that belonging to the Prince of Wales, and was thus taken there, rather than to the Prince of Wales. Another report states that he was invited on board of the Dom Afonso while in another of the boats but, whatever the detail, once on board this vessel it seems, his head swelled a little as so much praise at his heroics was bestowed upon him by the high social class of folk on board including the could-have-been-king-of France had there not been a successful, anti-monarchist revolution with a somewhat democratically elected Government replaced rather undemocratically by a dictatorship three years later. And there were some rather charming ladies on board, one of whom was the could-have-been-queen-of-France, and another, the nearly-Empress-of-Brazil, who might have been a little affected by the sight of a naked, or undressed enough to be considered naked, man who had exhibited bravery as much as he might have been exhibiting the evidence of his pudenda like a ballet dancer or the hugging lycra of an athlete.

There is a different version of Frederick's conduct after those final moments and his financial status had been misunderstood by those who considered him merely as a poor blue jacket, as sailors were colloquially referred to. Once eventually back on board his own ship the New World climbing up from the boat after his brief sojourn on the Dom Afonso, it was claimed by the captain that Frederick Jerome had said that he didn't need to work anymore such were the rewards he had received on board the Dom Afonso and the rewards he could subsequently expect, 'I'm a gen'l'man now, sir. I've got plenty of money. I don't want to work anymore. I'll go in the cabin now.' Whether this was the conceit of tongue in cheek or not, doesn't come across well and the Captain and, it appears his shipmates didn't take kindly to it, whether through jealousies or the abuse of the negation of their own heroic roles in the rescue. Captain Knight interviewed all the men individually and they virtually all had the same story. It transpires that all the men acted with equal bravery and Jerome was singled out as a lone hero only because he had told his story on the Dom Afonso like a fisherman's tale and this was the one that was believed. Inspired by some beautiful women of high social standing his story would quite understandably have had a little exaggeration within its content. It seems that it was considered that any of the men could have shinned up the ropes, but it was Jerome who was ordered to, perhaps because his previous demonstration of selfless bravery in a former shipwreck, was known to all. However, on the Dom Afonso, his head had seemed to swell a bit, for which he can take little blame. He had succeeded in being equal to folk of higher society, higher than he could ever have hoped to achieve through his status as a simple blue jacket and they were people of this otherwise unattainable high social status for a man like himself and his shipmates, and who had waited upon his every word.

These last survivors from the Ocean Monarch had been immediately taken to the Prince of Wales, dried and clothed. In the confusion of accounts, it was perhaps from here, if he had arrived here first, and perhaps with a drop of spirit within him, that Frederick Jerome was ready to go back to the New World, but instead it was likely that he was cordially asked to board the Dom Afonso where the esteemed company of military mindset, in which brave deeds were expected, desired to praise his bravery. On board here the effusion of human kindness had been poured upon the survivors, most especially by Mr and Mrs Lynn of the Waterloo Hotel in Liverpool. The survivors, as they had been hauled onto the vessel, were dried and clothed, as most were virtually naked and Mrs Lynn hugged and comforted the children as they were brought to her. One of the survivors, Mary Sales was taken in by the Lynns. She had lost her brother, husband and other family members. She settled in to the Waterloo Hotel in Liverpool and remained there with the Lynns for some long time afterwards.

The parts played by the Princess de Joinville and the Duchess D'Aumale on the Dom Afonso, in looking after the survivors, especially the children, who were more dead than alive, were emphasised by the Vice Consul Joao Francisco Froes. Princess de Joinville, as sister to the Emperor, had been heir to the throne of Brazil but her sister in law had given birth on 19th July of this year and so she would not be the successor after all. All the ship's contingent parted with their spare clothing and presented it to those in most need. The Dom Afonso then brought the passengers, a hundred and forty five in all, to the Sloyne in the Mersey where most were landed and then transferred to the President steamer and taken to the pier head across the estuary at Liverpool. This was nearest to the Northern Hospital to where those suffering from burns and severe contusions, some heavily bandaged, most almost nude, could be conveniently admitted. The walking wounded or the largely physically unscathed, were found accommodation overnight at the workhouse or wherever suitable accommodation could be found. For those that hadn't survived, but whose bodies were picked out of the water or who had died on board any of the rescue vessels, they were put in the dead house at the end of the dock, a building for the purpose of placing in it those unidentified bodies regularly washed ashore from parts unknown, or picked out of the dock itself.

Two other ships observed at the scene of the tragedy, the Cambria and the Orion did not turn towards the stricken ship in order to give any assistance, but sailed on instead. Signals allegedly given from the Cambria were not seen by the frigate, and in the confusion of the rescue many reports are misinterpreted. Both had left Bangor and had passed within five or six miles of the Ocean Monarch. The Cambria had noticed the ship on fire after passing Puffin Island. There was much controversy as to whether if the ships had gone to the assistance that many more lives could have been saved. As it was subsequently learnt, there was more than one ship named either the Cambria or the Orion and a disclaimer was published in the Liverpool Standard from the companies that owned ships of the same name. These mistakenly reviled ships of the same names at the time had alibis and were not the vessels in question as they were many miles away from the scene at the time, one in Glasgow and the other at the other side of the Atlantic. Captain John Hunter of the steam ship Cambria, the one that was at the scene and who did not give assistance when it seemed he was able and obliged to do so, explained that he had not sufficient coal to proceed to the Ocean Monarch and get back to Liverpool as well, since he had given away much of his coal while at Bangor. Unaware that it was a migrant ship he thought that since there were many other vessels in the area giving assistance to the ship, his own assistance wouldn't be needed. With a responsibility to his own vessel and some hundred passengers and livestock, had he gone to the assistance he would have had to wait for a supply of coal in order to get back to Liverpool, and the seas being as they were he would be putting both passengers and cargo and the ship itself in too much danger.

The role that the Cambria and the Orion played, or didn't play, in the incident was scrutinised at the inquest with charts and the relative positions of the ships to each other and the burning ship. Both ships were exonerated as well as their captains, as well as captain Murdoch himself (and it seems that his namesake, the first officer captain Murdoch on the bridge of the Titanic on the night of that disaster, in taking avoiding action, cannot be blamed that by taking that action, on subsequent analysis it might have been the wrong thing to do in the circumstances but the only right thing to do at the time.)

The jury at the first inquest was out for a quarter of an hour only, and returned a verdict of accidental drowning, exonerating the captain of the Ocean Monarch but also disapproving, in the first instance, the lack of action by the two vessels Cambria and Orion.

It would be a while before these two criticised vessels would be able to tender their explanations and justifications. The exhaustive proceedings had lasted until nearly 9.30pm.

THE END OF THE RESCUE

It was after three o'clock when the Queen of the Ocean, replete with rescued passengers, unable to do any more, left for Liverpool. When it had left, there were just a few small boats gallantly tossing about by the side of the Ocean Monarch and bringing off the few remaining passengers. The first mate Jotham Bragdon had been there from the first to the last. One report of an English observer states that an unidentified man, only described as a 'foreigner', also stayed to the end, clinging to the side of the vessel aiding the frightened passengers down to the boats, until there was no-one left on the vessel. He would have been observing Frederick Jerome though maybe he described him as foreign because perhaps it was below the dignity of an Englishman to be seen in such a state of undress which would say more about the observer and a potential xenophobia than the man intimately involved without being encumbered by the self-consciousness of dress sense, in the rescue. He was not a foreigner, such is the preconception of national identity, but an Englishman albeit living in America and sailing on an American ship. By the time the rescue had been completed and the last vessels began to make their way to their various ports of destination, the Ocean Monarch was burnt almost to the level of the water line, a blackened and smoking hulk on the surface.

The last person had been taken off the boat in this way at about 3pm, though exact times differ, and these last passengers would have endured three hours of little hope and only full of the expectations of death while the flames burned furiously and ever increasingly towards them and the sea, their potential saviour also, would be more likely to drown them if they were to jump in.

When all passengers were deemed to have been saved, the Dom Afonso had brought up its anchors and towed the boats of the New World until they could be released to regain their parent vessel. This would be the time when Frederick Jerome would have stepped out of his fantasy world and into the stern reality of the critical gaze of his shipmates. When this had been achieved, the two outward bound vessels, the New World on its way to New York, and the Prince of Wales for Bangor, continued to their destinations. The yacht, Queen of the Ocean, was one of the boats that stayed until about three o'clock and when then there was nothing else that could be done it made for Liverpool arriving there about 7pm., where anxious crowds awaited in the dock for news of friends and relatives. After the tears and hugs and man hugs for those who were reunited, would then begin the most awful but necessary task for those who had to identify bodies in the dead house or make the journey to other inquests where the bodies had been washed ashore all along the coasts.

A similar reunion would have been witnessed as the naval frigate anchored in the Sloyne and discharged its rescued passengers to the ferry across the Mersey. In the words of the Liverpool Mercury of October of that year asking the question, 'What is a lifebuoy?' and demonstrating the fact that the Ocean Monarch only appeared to have a single one with which a single man was rescued several miles from the ship which, if many of these had been available then many more survivors would have been picked out of the sea alive and 'Instead of friends in Liverpool being paralysed by the receipt of the cold, dead bodies of those they had just a few hours before kissed and held by the hand in all the vigour of health and warmth of hopeful life, they might have rejoiced in congratulations on a happy escape.'

The Liver steam tug stayed by the vessel until she went down in a further assurance that there was no-one left on board or floundering in the sea. It was about thirty yards from the burning ship as it finally sunk which was now burnt down almost to deck level as if it had been deliberately 'carpented' that way. 'The sea first made its way onto the after part of the ship; and as she gradually settled herself into the bosom of the deep, large volumes of flame, with a hissing and crackling noise, rushed into the air, till at length, being completely engulphed, she disappeared in about fourteen fathoms, causing a heavy swell for a moment. When the sea became settled, nothing was seen of the wreck save a few pieces of burnt timber and some spars floating near the spot.' (Caledonian Mercury Aug 31st 1848).

It was also stated in one report that the lifeboats from the Point of Ayr (North Wales) and Hoylake set off at 3.15pm which is a bit late, for by that time the ship was all but burnt out. But then while it took only seconds to signal news across from Wales to Liverpool, it would have taken longer, without a structured telegraph system in that part, to get a message down the coast to Point of Ayr, the fastest being on horseback or likewise from Liverpool and across the estuary and another stretch on horseback to Hoylake.

THE BODIES

The dramatic demise of the Ocean Monarch was sensational news, as much as the Titanic or the Lusitania, in peacetime or quasi peacetime respectively, and other maritime tragedies would engender on the destruction of each in its turn in the popular imagination. And there are plenty of reports and eye witnesses and, in the confusion of events, understandably conflicting in fact here and there.

Of the ship's contingent of steerage passengers numbering 322; second cabin 22; first cabin 6; crew 45; and a doctor, 132 people were saved by the Queen of the Ocean, 156 were taken on board the Dom Afonso by the boats scurrying to and from the burning ship. The smack picked up 13 (other reports state 17 and then again 16) and the Prince of Wales 17. 209 passengers arrived in Liverpool during the course of the day and a further 16 (or, another report; 20) were landed at Bangor by the Prince of Wales which was heading that way. Of the total contingent of about 399, it was estimated at the time that 170 must have been lost. Those that hadn't survived were, for some time after, as corpses, either picked out of the water or scattered along the beaches from Wales to Cumberland (Cumbria). Some nine of these were the bodies washed up on the shore of the Fylde Coast at Bispham and Norbreck, and were buried in Bispham Parish Church. Only one of these bodies, that of Alice Wrigley's, out of eight women and one man, was positively identified, as the bodies were laid out for a short period in the hope of recognition before burial. Some of the bodies picked up and given names do not appear on the passenger lists and amount to more than the 'four others' who are officially not named perhaps through clerical error, or late arrivals, or maybe the passenger lists had been, and maybe had always in fact been, less precisely or even carelessly, compiled.

The subsequent inquest would condemn the non-action of both the Cambria and the Orion for not going to the assistance of the Ocean Monarch when they were clearly in range, and could have reached the vessel at the same times as both the Queen of the Ocean or the Dom Afonso. It also condemned the crew of the Pilot Queen who wasted no time in scavenging what property they could from the unfortunate passengers instead of going to their assistance in their time of great need, despite the requests of the rescued passengers transferred to them, and who felt the threatened need to reward the three man crew of the vessel with cash and property for their accommodation on the boat. Many more lives it was claimed at the time, could have been saved if these three vessels had acted within the normal regulations of the sea. However, in the court case that followed, both the crew of the pilot boat were acquitted and eventually the true stories of the two maligned vessels came out.

Inquests were held on the bodies of those recovered and identified if identification was possible, and this took some time in individual cases and included exhumations and re-burials over the course of time. Some bodies would have had no-one to identify them, especially if whole families had been wiped out. Some were brought ashore who had died on the rescue ships or had been picked up from the sea. Other bodies were washed ashore at Hoylake and at Menai Bridge, as the sea distributed the bodies along these shores. The body of an unidentified four year old boy was buried at Llandysillio churchyard, a few miles from Bangor in North Wales. He had been picked out of the water alive, but probably barely alive, by the Prince of Wales steamer but died on board. This would have been later identified as the body of four year old Willy Jackson (reported in another newspaper as a 'fourteen year old boy' such is the confusion of reporting.) The nine that were washed up at Blackpool (or Bispham Parish of the day before Blackpool had been incorporated as a town and even shortly before it had even been given an identity and authority as a town) provide the substance which inspired this account. A single body, that of Alice Wrigley, has a gravestone. Originally from Bury, she was twenty six years old and married at nineteen years of age as a minor in 1841. She had been on her way to meet up with her husband in America who had evidently found work as an engineer in the cloth trade there. She was wealthy enough in her own right to have been able to afford a cabin berth and her family and husband also able to finance a gravestone to their wife, daughter and sister.

During the first week of September about fifteen bodies were washed up on this coastline identified as Blackpool, a developing watering place, fifty or so miles north of Liverpool and used to shipwrecks and giving aid to those who had been shipwrecked and left with nothing. There was little that could be done to these bodies apart from the attempt to identify them and give them a decent burial in the religious tradition of the day and expected legally by Act of Parliament. The distance to this Fylde coastline was not great. From this place, the hills of Wales can clearly be seen in the ordinariness of a clear day and the burning ship the Ocean Monarch was reportedly clearly visible though the distance too great to be able to observe the many ships passing along the busy sea lanes from there without a telescope. Just less than a hundred years later in 1942 the burning city of Liverpool could be seen not only from the fire watch at the top of the famous tower during the conflict of WW2 but also from the roof tops of Blackpool and in earlier in 1914, during conflict once more, the burning of the ship Vedra clearly seen at the tip of the Walney Island to the north in Morecambe Bay from the Promenade and the piers at Blackpool, flames reaching reportedly hundreds of feet into the air.

Elsewhere, bodies from the Ocean Monarch were brought to Hoylake, picked up by fishing boats and amounting to thirteen in number. There were two children less than two years old, a man about sixty years old, a lad, thirteen who was lame in the left ankle, a girl of about six or seven years old and who had on 'a black, velvet frock and trousers, the lower part tartan plaid'. Among these were eight women between twenty and sixty years old, two of them being identified as Joan Dunning and Mary Jones. The bodies were placed in the Punchbowl Hotel, cleaned and then covered in sail cloth until the coroner could attend and give his verdict. £22 6s (£22 30p; approx £1,800) was found in the clothing of one of the women. Any money that wasn't claimed was given to Mr Nielson, the elected treasurer of the fund for survivors. More bodies were washed up along the shores from Wales to the Lake District along the northwest coast of England.

Most bodies washed ashore over the coming weeks were badly decomposed. Those bodies washed up at Blackpool, and the smaller collection of houses known as South Shore further south, were described in detail in the newspapers in order to assist in identification. One was a 'portly' woman, fully dressed, in a large cotton plaid mourning dress, described as being in 'second' mourning and thus complying with the strict Victorian rules for women in mourning, the second mourning being the period after the first year of wearing black when other demure colours, not much different, could be worn to maintain the strict tradition. She had on also black, worsted stockings and black, stuff boots. She had a wedding ring on her finger with initials JC engraved upon it. The second lady was about forty three years of age and was still wearing her Dunstable bonnet, with a veil attached, typical of the image of a well to do woman of the age, and fully dressed in a blue 'hail showered print' dress, an over and an under petticoat and she had a red and white woollen plaid shawl. Also under her dress she wore a man's waistcoat. Her arms had been badly scorched perhaps indicating she had been holding onto the rigging for some time before having to let go. She also wore a wedding ring with the initials GW.

On the level of a physical playing field, the female of the species is always, it is perhaps evident, born into a natural pain and discomfort which persists for much or all of a lifetime, whereas the male usually has to go out and look for it, all being equal of course. In the case of one particular distressed female washed ashore at Bispham, not only had she been nearly burning to death, the alternative for which was to throw herself from a height, a fear in itself, into the dreaded fear of drowning, but she had also, if it had not been premature, reached her term and had been giving birth at the same time. It is trusted that the shock of hitting the coldness of the water and the extreme dread of the situation had rendered her unconscious and the unpreparedness of the birth was a natural result of extreme body shock. The two of them, mother and child, as corpses, arrived together on shore, where it is reported the foetus was still attached.

A third woman was 'tall and slender' with a 'fine head of auburn hair'. Her dress was a scarlet red of Orleans cloth and fitted up to the neck, again fitting a classic image of a female of the time. Beneath her dress she wore a white skirt and white, flannel petticoat and white socks. She had a couple of box keys around her neck, for boxes which would now be at the bottom of the sea off the Welsh coast many miles away or taken up from the water by the insensitive hands of scavengers. The fourth body was that of a young girl of about seven or eight years old wearing a green, plaid overcoat which was open at the front. Perhaps she hadn't time to throw it off on advice, or perhaps she was too scared to. She had on blue socks and a pair of new, ankle-strap shoes.

While dressed in all this attire, conventional on land in society, it is not conducive to swimming or surviving on the sea. If jumping into the sea out of necessity to avoid death by burning, or falling in accidentally without the time or the decision for one or the other options and, if fear might have taken away the ability to make a decision to divest of clothing, most in this kind of attire would have stood no chance at all unless picked up almost immediately.

The men washed up included an aged, bald man with only a shirt to his top, so he had discarded his jacket or topcoat, but he was wearing two pairs of trousers of 'fine cloth' which, it was deemed necessary to state, that they were buttoned up in front, and brown, kitted, worsted stockings. Another was the body of a sailor since he had on a blue, flannel shirt and blue, pilot cloth trousers and a pair of sailor's boots. In the leather belt around his waist, he carried a whittling knife. He was about thirty years of age and had long, black hair. Another was the body of a young boy about seven years old wearing jacket and trousers of drab, cotton cord, on which each knee had been patched with the same coloured material.

Further north at Norbreck where the longshore drift had carried the bodies that little bit further, four women were recovered. One of these had a scent bottle, a gold watch key and chain and several valuable rings in her pockets as well as 16s (60p; approx £64). She was wearing a pair of light blue jean stays over a purple, silk dress, white petticoat 'trimmed with lace', and a pair of cloth boots described as 'good'. Another woman, who was about thirty five years old was dressed in a brown silk dress had £3's worth of gold (£243.03p) and a shilling (5p; approx £2.00) in her pocket along with combs, a purse and wrist cuff. A third body was that of a young girl of about fourteen years of age.

These bodies would be interred as soon as possible, given time for possible identifications in the nearest and appropriate parish church at Bispham, but one was kept because it was understood that it would be identified by relatives. It was also understood that it might be the body of an Elisabeth Steele though the only identified body at the church on a gravestone or in the parish records, is that of Alice Wrigley. There isn't an Elisabeth Steele on the passenger lists so perhaps she was another of the unidentified 'four others', and maybe even one of Alice Wrigley's travelling party perhaps, if Alice might have been travelling in company.

A few miles further south from this shore, at Lytham, six bodies were cast ashore at the same time, three were women and there was one man and two boys. No particulars were given in the newspaper excepting that a ticket on one of the female bodies with the names of three passengers, James and Mrs Mantagh and their infant child, Jane was found. Another body of a female was washed ashore at Carr House near Rossall College at Fleetwood further north.

At Heysham, further north still, a man found the naked body of a young man on the shore near to his home. He was about eighteen years old and was of slight figure about five foot four inches (1.64m) in height, light brown hair and with manicured nails as if he was not used to hard work. It was suspected it might be the body a man called Coombs who hadn't yet been accounted for from the Ocean Monarch. The body had been severely beaten and it was supposed to have been bashed about by the rocks while it was in the sea. Another body was dressed in black and a letter in the pocket identified the name of John Curly who had relatives in Roxbury, Massachusetts. Perhaps he was American or perhaps he was visiting friends and family left behind or, perhaps again, he was emigrating to meet up with relatives and the start of a new life.

At Southport on the 8th September, with planks and debris from the wreck being washed ashore at every tide, among other bodies was that of a young girl of about fourteen years of age. She was wearing two petticoats, an under and an over, beneath a black cotton dress patterned with small white spots. Around her neck she wore a piece of ribbon with a Catholic bible attached to it. Her body was in such a poor state that she was buried straight away. Another woman was about thirty to thirty five years of age and was wearing a brown, worsted dress with silk flowers. She had a gold ring on her finger and in the purse in her pocket she had three shillings (15p; approx £12.00), in silver. Near her was another woman, described as stout and in her late forties. She had a twilled, worsted shawl and was wearing a brown, stuff dress under which were gingham petticoats. She had a gold locket in her purse with a lock of hair in it, and on her finger was a brass wedding ring. Her name was assumed to be Spencer from a piece of paper found in her pocket, though the only Spencer on the passenger list is Frances Spencer and she is described as being only twenty two years old. A female child about four years of age was wearing a blue and green, plaid coat dress and a white, holland pinafore. From one of her feet, a drab (ie of a light brown colour) cloth boot was missing, the other still attached.

A middle aged man of average height was the only male among this group. He was stout and dressed in a black frock coat, black waistcoat, check shirt and Wellington boots, and not a long time since they had been made fashionable by the Duke of Wellington himself. He had a red, silk purse in his pocket, two pocket books and a penknife, and £2 13s 7d (£2 60 approx £165.00) on his person. He was adjudged to be Daniel Pollard of Huddersfield.

Elsewhere, the corpse of a young man was picked up in the mouth of the Mersey and his pockets contained a knife, some keys, one or two trinkets, intimate relics of a close family association, and the name William Pawson was noted on a piece of paper with reference to a Leeds address. Enquiries determined that the body did indeed belong to William Pawson and identified by his father, Joseph Pawson of the White Lion Inn, Quarry Hill, Leeds. William was nineteen years old and is described as a shoe binder. He had been travelling with his wife and son and both were thought to have drowned. His sister Jane, who was travelling with him, also perished. Her body was picked up at Waterloo near Liverpool. Initially it was buried at Sefton nearby but was disinterred and moved to

Birkenhead where it was buried with her brother. The Pawsons are names also missing from the published passenger lists.

There was also, at another time, a male about sixty years old and about six feet (1.8m) tall dressed in a blue, pilot cloth coat with outside pockets, a blue, cloth waistcoat with a second, cotton quilted waistcoat beneath it. He also had low shoes, grey, worsted ribbed stockings and a flannel shirt. Another middle aged man, stout and also about six feet in height, was a little more fancifully dressed in a fancy striped, cotton shirt, fancy worsted waistcoat, cut fustian trousers, very large flannel drawers, laced shoes which it was stressed had six holes on each side and grey, worsted stockings. He had one shilling (5p; approx £4.00) in silver in his pocket along with keys, a penknife and pencils. Another body was that of a very stout female, about four foot six inches (1.37m) in height and she was wearing a pink, cotton dress, blue cotton petticoat, grey flannel petticoat, red neckerchief, black stockings, drab cloth boots, a ring on her finger and a necklace of blue beads. Half a sovereign (2s 6d; 12.5p; approx £10.00), 2s (10p; approx £8.00), two combs, two purses and a weaver's pick were found on her so, perhaps, she was from one of the cotton towns of Lancashire, towns soon to be put in dire straits with the blockades of the American cotton exporting ports of the South during the Civil War. The body of a young boy dressed in a black velvet frock coat was recovered from the beach at Thurstaston in the Wirral and was laid out in the church before an inquest and a respectful burial. The rector of the church, a reverend John Fish, wrote a letter to the Liverpool Standard on September 5th, just in case the parents, or a relative, may still be alive and that they could be assured he had received a respectful burial.

Three more bodies reveal a secretly contrived attempt at escape from circumstance on the Ocean Monarch which ended tragically in disaster and is exemplified in the lives of Mr Bacon the master, and Mrs Walter the school mistress, of St Luke's workhouse in Clapton,

London who left their families behind and eloped together hoping to reach America to start a new life together there. After an evident and lasting, earlier liaison between the two, the scheme between them was secretly put into action when Mr Bacon was first granted leave of absence from his job so he could settle some private matters and a few days later Mrs Walter was also granted leave of absence to visit a sick mother in Devon. Both had spouses and families which they deserted, though Mrs Walter took her youngest child with her as they left for Liverpool. Mrs Walter's husband, the schoolmaster of the workhouse, was in prison (the 'House of Correction') – for a misdemeanour described as exposing himself to 'respectable' women, revealing the stark division between a poor woman in rags in the workhouse who was vulnerable to abuse and the 'respectable' woman who wasn't in rags and who had no need of the workhouse and whom it was wrong to abuse yet both deserving of the same respect but not given it. So Mrs Walter didn't think her husband needed any fond goodbyes. He probably only found out when he was released from custody or, during his custody, by the cynical confidences of a vindictive warden. The children it is reported, were left with relatives who, perhaps with surprise if not in on the scheme, confirmed their departure after the event, when enquiries were begun on the disappearance of the two. It was to Mrs Walter's great disadvantage, and her secret would have been out sooner than she had expected, when her mother had arrived from Devon shortly after her daughter had left and, in perfectly good health as the sick relative that her daughter had claimed time off work to see to, and began enquiries about the whereabouts of her daughter. None of this group survived. Mr Bacon had £800 (£64,809.01p) with him so they would have had a good start at their destination had they made it successfully. His body, once identified, was disinterred from its grave where it had already been placed in Abergavenny, after it had been washed ashore there, and transferred to the Abney Park cemetery in Clapton,

London. A large crowd had gathered at the cemetery for the re-burial. Mr Bacon had been the master of the workhouse for a number of years and had already been to America, in his former occupation as a police officer, and had travelled widely there in order to hunt down the rate collector of St Luke's who had absconded with several thousand pounds of the parish money. Such is irony.

At Caernarvon on the 14th September an inquest took place on two older, male bodies picked up in the vicinity of the Orme Head. It was supposed that they were the bodies of Samuel Fielding and William Scamborough. Thirty nine sovereigns (£39; £4,747.33p) and a silver watch were found in the clothes of Samuel Fielding as well several tickets to ride which showed he was a passenger along with William and others. William Scamborough also had a silver watch on him and £11 (£891.12p). The verdict was that they were found drowned, with the recovered evidence demonstrating that they were passengers of the Ocean Monarch. Their effects were kept with the coroner so that they could be reclaimed by relatives. The identification of Samuel Fielding's body calls into question that he was the last man off the boat clutching the child to him. If he was indeed the last man off the boat he would have been one of the rescued. Other reports claim that most of the remaining passengers on the front of the ship were women and children and it was a woman who was the last off the boat with the child, and which would appear more likely. Then there is a Samuel Fielding in the list of the rescued so it is probable, whether he was first or last off the ship, that a body had been incorrectly identified as his. The name of William Scamborough is another that is not present on the published passenger list.

At Liverpool on 16th September the body of thirty eight year old Richard Cumming, a steward, found by the Cambria, legitimately in the area at the time, floating near to the northwest lightship, was identified by his wife Charlotte. The inquest returned a verdict of accidental death.

At Formby on the evening tide of the 7th and the morning tide of the 8th September several bodies had been washed up. The first was described as a 'black man', about fifty years old, and probably by his clothes and his skin colour, was one of the stewards on board the ship. He was about five foot nine inches (1.8m approx.) in height and dressed in black cloth trousers, a blue flannel shirt, blue stockings and strong shoes. An55other man was about thirty years old, a little taller at 5 foot 11 inches and dressed in a black, cloth coat, light brown knee breeches and leggings. He had a blue and white striped vest, dark blue stockings and laced boots. He carried in his pocket a comb, key and an address card of a lodging house in Dublin Street Liverpool, presumably where he had stayed during his last night on shore before sailing.

Also there was a man about twenty six years old and about 5' 10" high, dressed in black cloth trousers and vest and a fine, linen shirt. This man had been quickly identified as the son of Joseph Bladen, an engine fitter of Birmingham.

A girl of about sixteen years of age, about four foot four inches high, (1.5m approx) completely nude and possibly one of those who were lying on the beds due to sea sickness with little time to wake, realise what was going on, and dress properly before getting up to the relative safety of the deck, rushing, or being dragged up there with a loose covering quickly thrown over her body. Another woman of about forty five years old was dressed, and in a brown merino dress, black stockings and low, strong shoes. She had 3 shillings (15p; approx £12.00) and a farthing (approx 8p) in her pocket and a ticket for the voyage with the name Winifred Keogan and Rosey Mulrooney on it. The jury at the inquest for these bodies sat at Southport and recommended that ships of this nature should carry sufficient firefighting equipment.

At New Brighton on the other side of the River Mersey from Liverpool, Mr Churton the coroner conducted an inquest on a man found drowned and presumed to be from the Ocean Monarch. He was about thirty five to forty years of age and was wearing a brown, Oxford tweed shooting coat and blue trousers and a neckerchief 'presumed to have been red', so had probably lost its colour by its soaking in the water. About the same time the body of a woman was picked up by the Vale of Clwyd steamer, again presumed to be from the Ocean Monarch. She was five foot high (1.5m) and 'apparently' pregnant. She was wearing cotton drawers, black petticoat, a black stuff apron but no outer dress, again perhaps startled from her bed by the panic. She had a plain gold ring on her finger. The verdicts, as in all these cases, were 'found drowned'. Some of these bodies were buried at Christchurch, and this presumably the Christ Church in Liscard, Wallasey, a little further up the road from New Brighton itself.

From Wisbech at the other side of the country in Cambridgeshire, came the news that two of its residents had sailed on the Ocean Monarch. For Mrs Gilliat ('daughter of the late Mrs Morriss') and formerly of the town, it was reported that she had witnessed the 'heart-rending destruction' of her three children and had ultimately perished herself while returning to America on the Ocean Monarch, but they turned up safe and sound in America having made their way on a different ship. However, tragedy was determined to strike her as, on a visit to her daughter who had married while she was away, she fell ill and died. Her brother also, soon after, was 'struck with insanity'. She leaves four children and her husband in Cleveland Ohio. Private tragedies run parallel with collective tragedies but often don't get the same publicity or the same collective sympathies unless there is some drama attached.

The Cambridgeshire paper is aware that, of several parties from Sleaford in Lincolnshire, some had survived and some had succumbed to this 'awful and unparalleled casualty.' The other local resident, the 'lady' of Dr Anderson, presumably his wife, as she was formerly Miss Hardwicke, and on her way to join her husband was lucky to survive as she was rescued. She was twenty four years old but there is no mention of her five year old son, Thomas, being among the survivors. On the 5th September Joseph Lister was waiting in Boston (America) for his brothers and sister, Thomas, James and Mary Ann, to join him from Sleaford in Lincolnshire to start a new life in America but when the news of the disaster of their ship reached him, and assuming his siblings had drowned, he was so distraught that he fell ill and died of 'brain fever'. The tragedy was that his siblings had survived the disaster having been rescued from the ship.

In September too, at Llandudno the body of a female was washed ashore. All she was wearing was a calico chemise and a coarse, black, merino gown and again probably in bed when the panic started. There was nothing on the clothes to determine the name, and the body was so decomposed that it was impossible even to guess at the age. Mr Hope Jones, the deputy coroner held the inquest and her remains were buried in Llandudno churchyard.

An inquest at Menai was conducted by the coroner for Anglesey, William Jones, on the bodies brought there by the steamer, Prince of Wales. The Prince of Wales itself was delayed in its departure until the inquest had finished as it was taking the survivors back to Liverpool. It was assumed that the little girl in the comfort of a woman and who was only known as Lissie, was a sister of one of the deceased who had been a subject of the inquest. Lissie was reunited with her mother and siblings at the Northern Hospital. Once more the joyous content in the immeasurable sentiment involved in such a reunion was witnessed at the Hospital. Like many families the man had gone to seek work across the Atlantic and the mother and children were on their way out to join him. There were three other children on board who it seems were not so lucky to be reunited with their families. It is hoped that they were saved from the workhouse. When that old shipwrecked mariner's son had left for America the following year on the Guy Mannering, there is no evidence of his wife travelling with him. He left behind him a young daughter who at fifteen years old was soon, through ill health, admitted to the Union workhouse, an establishment with the unsavoury reputation of being the largest brothel in the city. Many of the folk returning to Liverpool were injured with burns especially to the hands, bruises and other injuries associated with the desperate struggle to survive. The druggist on board the ship, a Mr Thomas, had stayed up much of the night administering to the sufferers.

Bodies were brought to the dead house at the end of the Prince's Dock. The steam tug Skerrevorre brought five bodies, a man, two women and two children. Other fishing vessels picked up bodies and still more were distributed along the shores of North West England. Most of the bodies were bruised as they had been buffeted against the sides of the ship or by a desperate jump into the water or hit by heavy floating timbers in the strong swell. Many of the bodies had been scorched.

The bodies of those not collected from the water were found washed up on the shores of wherever the currents or longshore drift would take them. From the shores as far away as the Fylde Coast where the body of Alice Wrigley, and many others, were washed up, both the coastline of Southport and the hills of the Welsh Coast are clearly visible and, on a clear day, with some detail added the flames of the ship's demise were also evident, though the unfolding tragedy and the terror being experienced would be unknown to the casual, and perhaps curious, observer.

The body of a man, the first to be washed up on the Fylde shore line, as the winds had changed from south and south east to south westerly and which are the prevailing winds for the coast, and the cause of the many shipwrecks along its length, settled on the shore opposite the Royal Hotel, close to what is now the famous Blackpool Tower and proved a curiosity to view as much as a relic from the Titanic might be today. Laid out in an outhouse of the workshop of Mr Walmesley, a plumber and glazier, living in St Anne's Square in the town, it proved to be the morbid sensation that many folk made a purpose visit to look upon it. Blackpool was a dirty place at the time, overcrowded with day trippers and not enough accommodation for those who wanted an overnight stay. There was no running water or sanitation and the blood of the butchers' trade ran freely in one of the few laid out streets to be carefully avoided by the thousands of feet that trampled along its length. Though this would soon change for the better, and Blackpool would become a place full of curiosities to be seen or experienced, in this sense the decomposing corpse could perhaps be considered the very first attraction of its kind in the township that would develop as Blackpool and, along its Golden Mile, would achieve the title of the entertainment capital of the land, and later a place of refuge in times of national emergency. Though while there would be, in the future, many gross curiosities on display, they would not all be to do with dead bodies.

At Heysham, the acting coroner refused an inquest on two more bodies washed up there as this, in principle, had been dealt with at Blackpool and other towns, thus denying the potential identification and closure for any relatives, and is criticised in the newspaper for his denial. All that could be surmised was that the two bodies were of the lower working class because of their clothing and thus, perhaps, not important enough to bother.

Elsewhere, the bodies of two females and a man were picked out of the water in early September. The first of the females was found near the Crosby lightship and was much burnt and disfigured. She had black hair and was about 5 feet 5 inches in height. She was wearing a plain coloured merino dress and a flannel petticoat, but had no shoes or stockings. Perhaps she had been resting when the alarm was raised or perhaps she had taken them off before her audacious but necessary jump into the sea. The other female body was found floating near the Bell Buoy and was likewise disfigured. She was wearing a dark, stuff dress and a dark, quilted petticoat, a blue cotton apron with white spots and a white cap, shoes and black stockings. The body of a man was found floating in the River Mersey by the Prince's Dock basin. A pen case, a memorandum book and a book entitled 'The Farmer of Inglewood Forest', a book published by the writer Elisabeth Helme in 1795 and recently as 1846 performed as a play at the Royal Pavilion Theatre London, so it might have been quite a topical read. A copy could be bought for 10d (approx 4p; £3.30p) in 1847 (or earlier serialised in the newspapers for 1d (less than ½p) a copy. A contemporary of Jane Austen, Elisabeth Helme was a writer of independent ideas and included acute social issues in her novels. These novels, though proving popular at the time of their publication, didn't achieve the lasting popularity of Jane Austen's works. An interesting fact is that one of her books was the most read novel in Brazil at the time, having been translated into Portuguese, but it is not known whether any of the literate and Portuguese speaking folk on the Dom Afonso had read it. The man was evidently prepared for the long haul and had maybe already enjoyed a page or two in the comfort of a first or second cabin. He was evidently keen to record his momentous journey in his notebook, a journey which sadly did not continue after its first, brief chapter, and any preliminary notes perhaps washed out by immersion in the salt water. Like all the other inquests, this inquest concluded that these bodies were 'Found Drowned'.

Bodies continued to be washed ashore all along the coast from Wales to Cumberland and inquests, if the coroner didn't happen to be a bit lazy, and only the one was it seems, were held on all the bodies. Once brought ashore they were found a suitable place if a 'dead house' was not available. There was a dead house at Rhydland on the Abergele coast near Rhyl where the body of an unidentified male, who was assumed to be a labourer by his attire of check shirt, corduroy trousers and velveteen coat. His hands were very much scorched with the skin entirely peeled off one finger, revealing the bone. In his pockets were found keys, buttons, a knife and a receipt for his travel for which he paid £4, (£324.05p) representing a steerage berth (Number 383, berth 17). It is not known whether his last moments were spent in pure self-preservation, in cowardice or in the selfless attention to others in need. There were no witnesses identifiable to bear witness to his actions.

Johanna Tobin was one of the survivors and there is a Johanna Tobin who, later in the year, made it over to America only to die of consumption (TB) in hospital in New York in 1850 aged thirty five though, on the passenger lists, it is Honora her sister who is thirty four and Johanna the youngest at twenty six, if the passenger lists can be assumed to be acutely accurate. She had probably nothing to go back home for and, as it turns out, though unbeknown to her, little to look forward to. There is no record of her sister Mary's burial despite the body having been found and identified, nor do we learn of her other surviving sister Honora who was travelling with them and whether she decided to travel to America again or whether she stayed at home to be thankful for or regret the life she had been allowed to possess within her and the future she been allotted by the tragic circumstances of that late August day.

Luckier were Mr James Booker a sixty one year old farmer of Bent's Green, Eccleshill near Sheffield. He was with his adult son and daughter. They lost everything they had apart from their lives and the clothes they had upon their bodies. Mrs Booker had stayed at home. She was unexpectedly reunited with her son and daughter, Edwin and Mary a few days after they had left her. They had stayed alive due to their presence of mind and gritty determination. Twenty seven year old Miss Mary Booker (the passenger list gives her age as twenty four) was lowered into the sea by her father and brother, eighteen year old Edwin, tied to a rope. The sea was dashing about and the boat was pitching violently. Her father and brother followed. Drenched to the skin, her brother reached a waiting boat first and then Mary was hauled into it with some difficulty by her brother in an exhausted state. The family were some of the very fortunate ones who were taken to the Dom Afonso and afforded the basic comforts of its generosity. Mr Booker had hauled himself down by a burning cable and burnt his hands badly. Dragged into another of the boats, he was taken to the Bangor packet, Prince of Wales before being transferred to the Dom Afonso, probably due to his heart rending pleas to be reunited with his children and the readily available generosity of spirit of those many assisting the survivors.

At Caernavon on the 10th September two bodies were picked out of the water by the steamer Cambria. There was nothing on the bodies to identify them but one had over £39) worth of gold wrapped in a cloth belt around the waist and both had silver watches. The other had £11, (£4,747.33 and £1,338.99 respectively of the two amounts). When the fire was discovered, the first line of panic for many was to recover valuables. There was no thought of dying in that first moment and if you were going to survive you might as well survive with some wealth rather than nothing whatsoever. Perhaps one person in a family group collected the family and one person was allocated to save the material valuables. Those relative few that had any.

More bodies were washed up on the Welsh coast and described in the newspapers in the hope that someone might be able to identify them. A young woman washed up on the shore near Prestatyn was probably a cabin passenger as she was of 'respectable' appearance. She had on drawers, which might make her respectable, flannel petticoat and possibly a nightgown frilled at the sleeves, but no shoes or stockings and was perhaps resting at the time of the calamity with no idea of danger whatsoever in her imagination. She was also wearing a large diamond ring on the forefinger of her left hand, a ring was that was now in the possession of the parish clerk for safe keeping.

Five more bodies were picked up and taken to Rhyl, close to the tragedy.

The body of a 'coloured' man named Cummins was picked up by the Welsh steamer Cambria near the spot where the tragedy occurred. Perhaps he was the cook who had jumped overboard with a barrel as a hopeful float to keep him alive. 'Coloured' of course represents the perception of those of 'colour' being different from the norm which was considered white. Perhaps if he and his 'coloured' shipmates were American nationals they would belong to the North and would have a semblance of freedom. While the idea of slavery that would be the major cause of conflict in a little more than a decade's time in the land that the emigrants aspired to gain for their own perception of opportunity and freedom, and the grandson of the old shipwrecked seafarer called up to the army when New York was threatened by the approach of the menacing advance of the southern armies before the bloodshed of Gettysburg, relationships between the two forms of colour, and all the in between colours, in the city itself were nevertheless beset with a deep confusion of human identity, most especially by the lighter of the colours.

As well as the nine bodies from the Ocean Monarch washed ashore in the parish of Bispham, now part of Blackpool, and given the respect of a decent burial, even though just one body, that of a cabin passenger could be identified, three bodies, two women and a male child, were washed up as far north as Silverdale in the south of the Lake District on the 8th September.

As ships and boats picked up bodies and brought them ashore, and the bodies that were washed ashore, cleaned clothed and identified if possible and buried, the effects of any value in most cases anywhere were declared to the authorities in case there was a surviving member of the family who could claim them.

Altogether, about one hundred and seventy passengers and some crew lost their lives to the 'briny deep'.

THE INQUESTS

The first inquest was conducted by the Liverpool coroner, Mr Curry, on the five bodies that were brought there, and his ultimate verdict at the end of the inquest was, 'That the deaths of the five individuals were accidental, caused by drowning, in consequence of the ship Ocean Monarch taking fire; and that at the same time the jury would show their marked approbation of the conduct of the captain, and particularly that of the first mate, during that most trying scene, as also the noble and praiseworthy efforts of the distinguished individuals who signalised themselves at the awful catastrophe, as well as the officers and men under their command. Further we wish to express our disapprobation of the conduct of the masters of the two steamers Orion and Cambria, who might, we are led to believe, have rendered most efficient service to the ill-fated people on board.' This was the honest conclusion of this, the first inquest, and there were many more inquests yet to be arranged and completed as more bodies and more evidence accrued in the coming days and weeks.

There had been much evidence to gather in the first instance which had caused it to have been adjourned after the first day. The five bodies of this first inquest would initially represent all those who had lost their lives and the circumstances that caused the tragic destruction of the vessel. It was a packed house with representatives and solicitors of all concerned as the accuracy and truth of claims and accusations and counter claims and counter accusations had to be established and their truths determined.

Charles Locke, James Chiene and W P Gibbs were all seaman on board the Ocean Monarch and each exonerated the captain who was ultimately relieved of any blame. James Chiene claimed he had been shipwrecked for the third time in twelve months, merely passing his misfortunes off as a hazard of the job. He had been on board for two hours before he had no option but to jump overboard. He was able to reach and cling on to a floating spar until picked up by a boat and taken to the Dom Afonso. Charles Daniels Locke was an American seaman, and was one of a line of bucket men passing buckets of water at the Captain's orders, and supervised by the Captain in order to put out the fire as the evidence of James Chiene testified. He, like the captain, had eventually to jump overboard when the fire was only ten feet away from him. When he jumped overboard on seeing the second boat lowered into the water, he missed it and was ten minutes in the water before regaining the Ocean Monarch. Once up the rope and back on board a little further away from the fire, he helped in taking down the topgallant spar and, throwing it overboard, went over after it and clung on to it until eventually rescued by the boat from the Dom Afonso. He thought that if the crewmen had stayed at the fore of the ship and helped the women and children down by the ropes, many more could have been saved by the boats which had come to the aid of the ship. Women of course, he was not able to point out in the mindset of the day, are not incapable creatures, but in the dress of the day perhaps more handicapped than a man to make an escape down a rope, untrained, unprepared and for the first time in their lives.

As usual, in the calmness of the room in which the inquest took place, there was nevertheless the desperation to find a reason for the loss of human life on such a large scale and in such a dramatically tragic event, and a scapegoat was sought out to reach a conclusion and give an explanation. This at first had landed on the head of Captain Murdoch and he was the first to receive the backlash. To counter this, letters were sent out between all the concerned parties, exonerating the captain and praising those whose remarkable efforts assisted in saving so many lives and, published after the event, the truths had taken some time to be revealed.

At a Parliamentary level, the Chancellor of the Exchequer promised a full enquiry though this was hindered due to the fact that the ship was not a British ship and thus not under the jurisdiction of the British Parliament.

It was not the only duty of the inquest to determine the cause of death, which in most cases appears to be drowning since, to avoid death by burning, most had jumped into the sea to escape the fire, but it was also the duty of the inquest to determine the circumstances leading up to the fire for, 'A party having charge of a ship was compelled by law to use every exertion to protect his ship and the lives of those on board'. While the ship was American, there were those restrictions applying to a full enquiry by a British Government, nevertheless Captain Murdoch was under scrutiny and he attended along with the solicitors for all the commercial agents involved in the ship. The law as quoted at the inquest states that, 'Whoever shall by force prevent or impede any person endeavouring to save his life from any ship or vessel which shall be in distress, or wrecked, stranded, or cast on shore, whether he shall be on board or shall have quitted the same, shall be guilty of felony.' This is what Captain Murdoch was up against. However the positive result of the inquest evidently hadn't quashed the popular belief that the captain was entirely at fault. In a local newspaper article of 1883 concerning a stroll around the hamlet of Bispham, and in particular the parish church, the gravestone of Alice Wrigley was featured along with a story of the shipwreck which was in stark contrast with the true events as recorded at the time, nearly forty year earlier. Here the captain was even accused of opening the hatches to allow a free flow of air to fuel the flames and was blamed for the entirety of the disaster and the high number of casualties, all of who could have been saved if he had acted properly. Such is the longevity and tenacity of popular belief when it has a need for its own truth only.

THE DEE PILOT, QUEEN OF CHESTER

While there were acts of great bravery and self-sacrifice, there was also the other side of the human coin on show. Two Welshmen, John Benison and Thomas Bethell, owners of the Dee Pilot which had picked up some of the first survivors delivered by Jotham Bragdon off his little boat, were in the police court in Liverpool for allegedly robbing those who had been transferred to them. It was alleged that they had demanded 1s (5p; about £6) from every survivor they took on board. A blanket was taken from one of the survivors and he had to buy it back with his expensive lever watch. Another passenger was detained on the boat, after the others had been safely landed, because he had a lot of money on him. A seaman's trunk from the Ocean Monarch, thought at first to belong to a Richard Young of Portsmouth, Virginia was picked out of the water and forced open and robbed. The trunk was found at the home of John Benison. The three crew (the third member doesn't get a name in the accusations) in the vessel were accused of sailing around as much as they could to collect what they could from out of the water and ignoring the fact that they could have rescued several survivors if they had pursued an expected course of selflessness rather than tack into one which would invite reprimand and the scorn of many.

Just where in the water an object was picked up depended upon which coast it was nearest and thus what authority should deal with it and it seems that this trunk had been found and retrieved somewhere along the Welsh coast. Though there was a right to salvage of some of the parts and equipment from the ship consisting of spars and other timbers, variously broken off and cast adrift, all sorts of accusations of theft went about as soon as a rumour had been started and these accusations even reached the extremes of murder itself, as it was alleged the two men had murdered one of the passengers for their own gain.

It took some time for any kind of truth to come out and a £10 (£1,217.26p) reward was offered for anyone with information on the whereabouts of the alleged murder victim, Joseph Sheard of Huddersfield. The truth came out when Joseph Sheard contacted the newspaper to declare himself alive and well. He had been well treated and had voluntarily given the men a half sovereign (50p or £60.87p) for their assistance after he was put on board another vessel, the Taliesin, bound for Liverpool. It is not disclosed whether he received the reward for denying his own murder and solving the case by presenting himself to the authorities.

The men had certainly benefitted from their role as rescuers, but if they had been true heroes they could have done more. They had saved some lives but perhaps could have saved many others at only a small risk to themselves and, once more, an incident reflected in the Titanic disaster where a vessel could have gone in among the floundering survivors in the water or collected them from the undersubscribed lifeboats, and a large enough vessel could have even taken them off the ship by sending down its own boats, when many hundreds of lives would have been saved.

The inquest at the Holywell Justice Room near Flint provided a more detailed account, and the two accused had by now a sympathetic defence. The box that had been hauled out of the water by them had been taken by cart to Messrs Mathers, Bagillt's leadworks where they wanted a 'respectable' man to open it. When it was opened by the carpenter, the contents were found to be 'very wet and offensive'. The carpenter vouched for the men's statements and described the opening of the box which was secured by a clenched nail when brought to him, and he had difficulty in opening it. The owner of the trunk from the Ocean Monarch was Richard Joner, 'alias Adam Joner', not the Richard of Young of Portsmouth as previously understood and reported, and who claimed that when the trunk was returned to him, several items of clothing were missing including a pair of dark striped trousers, a spotted, silk handkerchief and a white shirt belonging to a messmate. When the trunk had been opened, the accused had said he would take the box back to Liverpool and get his wife to wash the clothes and put them out to dry. Sailors were always competent multi taskers when on board and would make, mend, wash and dry their clothes among many other skills. However, when on land it seems that these skills suddenly dissipated and it was the wives that were obliged to do the washing and mending. It was here then, at his home, that the Liverpool detectives found the trunk, and the accusations went from there. From the adjournment of a second inquest they were bailed to reappear on £50 (approx. £6,000) each, and sureties of £25 (approx. £3,000).

The men were eventually sent for trial in Flint but were acquitted there and recovered £20 (£1,620.23p) each for false imprisonment from the two Liverpool detectives named as Tuck and Bates, who had accused and arrested them. The Liverpool 'detectives' were not policemen as it turned out, and appeared to have been acting privately, however publicly spirited, and it was adjudged that they thus had had no authority to do what they had done. The accusation of the two pilots having murdered a passenger had proved to be false when the passenger had turned up. Whether they had been acquitted regarding the alleged thefts because of the letter of the law, rather than the moral considerations of the incident, is not clear.

THE NEW WORLD ACCOUNT

The medals duly awarded and distributed for those who conducted the rescues out at sea, at first did not include those participants from the sister ship of the Ocean Monarch, the New World, nor did they consider the Ocean Queen because after the incident they had both made their ways to New York, and so their stories were not told in full until the return of the New World to Liverpool, in December when the Humane Society had to increase its distribution of medals. Indeed, in the beginning, Captain Knight of the New World had been falsely vilified for his lack of participation in the rescue attempt. It was claimed that it was only the chastising pleas of the crew that turned the captain's sentiment to convince the New World to assist in the rescue. It wasn't until news of his professional, compassionate and influentially practical part in the rescue had been conveyed back across the Atlantic that the real story was told. His story is recorded in the following year by one of his passengers, who had been booked on the Ocean Monarch but who was transferred to the New World at the last minute for an unknown reason.

The account by this American passenger, a Mr G W Bartlett was published in the American newspapers on the 4th April 1849. He recounts the day as being wet as he left his friends in London at Euston station to take the six hour rail journey to Liverpool. Arriving there and getting back the use of his legs, he sent his luggage on board. The ship could not sail until the next day because of the adverse winds but, as a cabin passenger, he settled down to supper at the Captain's table and made acquaintances with his fellow passengers. They were a group of well-to-do people and could find sufficient in common no doubt and, later in the evening, after G W Bartlett had reflected lyrically in his diary on England's green pastures and distinguished literary figures as he stood on the deck, the passengers would all resort to their state rooms for the comfort of the journey.

When it was time to sail, the steam tug pulled the New World away from the dock and out into the Mersey, leaving it to its own resources when it had reached the open ocean. When Mr Bartlett awoke on the early morning of the sailing, he went up on deck and watched another magnificent ship, the Ocean Monarch still being towed passed the Bell Buoy, and in this way the ship by the side of them gained distance upon them as he observed, perhaps even wishing he had been upon it himself.

The Ocean Monarch and the New World have been described as sister ships, regularly leaving the same transatlantic ports on the same day and quite naturally there was an air of keen rivalry. Both captains were highly competent but not averse to a professional competition that would bring out the best in them both. On deck G W Bartlett was joined by the 'dark eyed' daughter of Captain E Knight, and the magnificence of the sailing ship within sight of them was negated by that sense of rivalry, 'I hope that she will not beat us!' claimed the young girl, calling the merchantman a 'she', but her ship was destined for New York where many of its passengers might take a walk on the wild side where one day, 'he' would be a 'she' anyway, if only in musical lyrics. The Ocean Monarch was off to Boston a little further north up the coast from New York and closer than that city, but they would no doubt be in touch by sight and flag signal if necessary for much of the way.

Sometime later the New World tacked away from its rival having to deal with a stiff head wind. It was a sunny day but the wind that was blowing was cold. Many of the passengers were out on deck, rather than in their cabins or confined below in the steerage, to get the fresh air into their lungs to counter the sea sickness, and taking in the magnificent views of the Welsh coastline about ten miles away. G W Bartlett remembers somebody saying with curiosity, rather than alarm, that he thought that the Ocean Monarch, still visible in the distance, was on fire. They looked at the smoke but thought it would have been coming from a coal fired steamer somewhere behind it and out of sight. Then Captain E Knight came out onto the deck and, looking through his glass, calmly but firmly stated 'she is on fire' and immediately, all rivalry disappeared. The New World was then ordered to bear down upon the stricken vessel. The Captain would have expected the same reaction of immediate consideration of help from another ship towards his. All seafarers would. There would have been a rush of activity among the crew as the sails were adjusted to change the course of the vessel. There was a moment for G W Bartlett to sigh with relief, as he considered the smoke rising up into the sky as he had very nearly sailed on the Ocean Monarch himself. It was a stroke of luck that he hadn't. He had booked his state room in that ship but for some reason which he doesn't reveal, or perhaps wasn't even aware of, this booking was transferred to the New World. Perhaps he wasn't sure whether he was going to New York or Boston but, anyway, any thoughts he might have had of being on that ship would now have been willingly dispelled, even though the extent of the disaster was yet unknown to him as the curling smoke had not yet completed it description of the misery and heartache that was to be its conclusion.

As they drew nearer, by now dense volumes of smoke could be seen coming from the rear cabin and then flames could clearly be seen. Other vessels, a steamer, a yacht and a ship were bearing down upon the burning vessel. The fire became intense very quickly and the flames leapt into the air. The evident tragedy was now unfolding. Passengers could clearly be seen crowding to the front of the ship, or climbing the rigging or jumping overboard. It was the horror of horrors that no ocean traveller wanted to dream of never mind be a witness to.

By the time the New World was as near as it could safely get, the sea was littered with bodies, some alive some evidently dead. The Captain ordered the two ship's boats, one a lifeboat and the other an ordinary ship's boat, to be dropped and manned, the boatswain in the lifeboat and the second mate in the other, five men to a boat with as many oars as they could gather. It's assumed that the New World had more than two boats at the disposal of its recorded seven hundred passengers but probably in its contingent of boats, grossly insufficient to cope with an event like that presently happening to the Ocean Monarch.

The flames eventually caught the rigging and the sails, and those trying to climb out of the reach of the flames stood no chance as the flames burnt the base of the masts and they began to collapse, crashing onto the deck or into the sea crushing anyone that was unfortunate enough to be in their way. There was some relief with the watchers to know that the fear was no longer with those that had drowned and death had brought its peace.

The small boats were now at the ship's edge, struggling with the swell and those folk struggling in the water were clinging to anything that might float, even if it might be a dead body. After an eternity went by, there was only a frightened few, all women it seemed at the fore of the vessel, too terrified to jump. He recalls the action of the boatswain of the New World in climbing the ropes to rescue the women but his story is at variance with the last person to leave the vessel. While the story from the boats is that of Frederick Jerome eventually convincing the man and child to come down by rope, GW Bartlett has the last two people to leave as being a woman and child, too afraid to jump the twenty feet or so, but the truth probably lies in a bit of both reports. If she had been encouraged off by Frederick Jerome in the first place and lowered down on the ropes she would have met the water still attached to the rope. She was so close to the rescue boat and the encouragement of the crew and perhaps the shouts of Frederick Jerome above her and yet so far away at the same time. Sometimes she was lost under the waves and then she would resurface, fear and determination showing in her face in the instinct of survival, assisted by the need to save her child, trying to catch a breath, still with the child in her arms. The boat eventually reached her and she was dragged out of the sea at first with a boat hook and then with the eager arms of the rescuers in the boat along with her child to the sanctuary of the boat in a scene which is depicted on the medal issued by the Humane Society to all those brave seafarers who had risked their own lives in order to save the lives of others. She was wrapped in the woollen shirts of the men in the boat and she was taken to the safety of the mother ship where, only half dressed and only half alive, she and her child were hauled up onto the deck by anyone who could help and were immediately taken into the care of the surgeon. And when this last person to be saved from the ship had been transferred to safety, it was the turn of the sailors to board. They stood on the quarter deck, wet through, shivering and half naked and the whole of the passengers including the six hundred or so of the steerage, let out a loud and deafening cheer, 'louder than the roaring of the waves'. And then the second boat, the lifeboat arrived and the crew were given another loud and unforgettable ovation. From then on the Captain brought up the anchors and set the sails for the homeward journey to New York and the flames of the Ocean Monarch were still, though less evidently, visible in the increasing distance.

The New World sailed away having done all it could in the situation, but it sailed away with its account and only an unkind and incorrect story of a ship that callously sailed away without any offer of help, was left for those on shore to consume. It would be some while before the correct account of the rescue would return and its falsely vilified Captain exonerated.

Once in his home country, the Massachusetts Humane Society awarded medals to the value of $20 ($649.43) along with a certificate of thanks to third mate William Baalham and Thomas Forbes, boatswain of the New World. And medals worth $10 ($329.71) to the eight of the crew who manned the boats, named as William Strand, William Grove, George Roositer, Henry Curtis, William Johnson, Edward Coe, Edward Dugdale and Frederick Jerome. Frederick Jerome was considered with the same importance as the seven other men. $10 medals were also awarded to those equivalent men of the Ocean Monarch, namely William Warwick, William Roberts, Philander Stewart, Robert Glennining, Daniel Wilder and James Stockwell. It was considered in some quarters at this time in the USA that the bravery of Frederick Jerome had been greatly overestimated, a sentiment that was criticised in the British press who couldn't give him enough credit.

When the New World eventually, in the course of its regular Atlantic crossings, returned to Liverpool, Captain Knight was able to give the true account of the story and a different angle on the heroics of Frederick Jerome. From then on this different angle of looking at the events was made available and more medals and gratitude were presented or shown to those hitherto ignored by lack of correct information.

Despite being responsible for saving about sixty people from the ship, Captain Knight however declined this presentation of a gold medal presented by the Liverpool Humane Society. It wasn't disdain as he had done the same in America when the Massachusetts Humane Society wanted to present him with one. He regarded that he had done his duty and didn't want to take funds from a charitable society. A silver medal was however presented to Mr W E Baalham, (sometimes Baaslam, or illegible, in the newsprint) third mate of the New World, and senior officer in charge of the boats, £5 (£608.83p) to Thomas Forbes the boatswain and £3 (£365.18p) each to seven of the eight men that manned the boats. Frederick Jerome, the man of the event on which most news and credit was focussed, had already received notification of his award.

THE LIVING AND THE RETURN TO THE SHORE

When the various ships and vessels with their cargos of desperate and injured survivors returned to port, there were those survivors who were landed on the shore in Liverpool or across the estuary at Seacombe. Others would return to Liverpool later on had they been put on an outbound vessel. The larger vessels anchored in the Sloyne opposite Tranmere, an oil terminal of future years, and the passengers were transferred to the ferry to be taken across the river to Liverpool. Once on shore, it was the turn of the town dwellers to demonstrate a compassion that had been exhibited by those out at sea. Here the survivors received the kindness of the human being and not always a kindness inspired by the self-congratulation of those administering the kindness, but a general flux of naturally impromptu and compassionate involvement. At the jetties when the various boats discharged their crews and passengers, there were crowds desperately waiting for news of their relatives before the surviving passengers were distributed among the hotels, or found more permanent accommodation in the workhouse or whatever suitable accommodation was generously offered, specifically named as Regent Street, though including other streets at the northern end of the town, the Northern Hospital being the place for the injured who needed more immediate and lasting medical care.

Those people who would have waved them off in the morning or had said their goodbyes the evening before, perhaps with a tear in the eye, not expecting to see them again, would have normally been severely overcome and exceptionally relieved to be re-acquainted with them as survivors.

A committee was formed immediately as 'the people of Liverpool have ever been proverbial for their exertions in the cause of humanity', at least for the last forty years as the slave trade had ended, such are the weighted specifics of self-congratulation. While this accolade might have ignored the slave trade conducted from the port, its inhumanity might now have been forgotten or blamed on an older generation. The committee for this present humanitarian organisation consisted of the Mayor, Thomas Horsfall, Admiral Grenfell, Edward Rushton, James Price, Thomas Littledale, J Aspinall Tobin, Robert Osgood, Jacques Myers, Lieutenant Hodder and Charles Cottesworth, with Mr D Nielson as the treasurer, the one who would allocate the collected funds to be distributed. By the Saturday after the disaster, in less than two days, over £800 (£64,809.01p) in cash had been collected as well as large stocks of clothes and provisions. A little further inland the Earl of Derby at Knowsley started off a fund at £50 (£4,050.56p), and Lord Stanley at £20 (£1,620.23p), a fund which eventually rose to £90 (£7,291.01p).

Mr John Bramley Moore was the chief promoter of the generosity of the Liverpool merchants. He was a town councillor and privileged alderman, and a member of the docks' board and had a keen interest in the sea, overseeing the construction of several docks along the Mersey, one being named after him earlier in the tragic month of the Ocean Monarch's departure. He was eventually mayor of Liverpool later in 1848 and was then energetic in arranging the fetes and festivals to generate funds for the aftermath of the tragedy and to support those affected by it. By 1862, as MP for Lincoln, since he had not been elected for Liverpool, he was to give a speech on whether or not to recognise the Southern states of America and which included the sentence referring to the freedom which he and his wealthy compatriots enjoyed in their own land, 'Unhappily this freedom did not exist in America, for they had witnessed greater despotism there than in any country in Europe during any period of recent history.' While perhaps this was a vindication of his own Conservative politics which through its own kind of despotism had played its part in the unrest in Europe, it might be expected to demonstrate there were those places on earth, intimating his own country of domicile, and governed by the principles of his political ideals that were far superior to the land of freedom that many believed to hold the answer to the direct resolution of their miseries. It was spoken when the differences between the northern and southern states were in a state of bloody, military conflict with more violent action expected as the two armies manoeuvred tactically into position for battle. It was kind of out of the frying pan and into the fire that some of those survivors of the Ocean Monarch who elected to resume their journey to America on the other ships would have had to experience.

John Bramley Moore also had a Brazilian connection, having lived in Rio de Janeiro for some years, so he might have had a dual language conversation over a glass of wine in the company of the contingent from the Dom Afonso while they were staying in Liverpool.

While the generosity of the Liverpool merchants was eulogised, it was also regretted elsewhere that the merchants of Dublin had not contributed a penny when many of the sufferers, actually nineteen out of twenty it was claimed, perhaps with a little exaggeration, were Irish. Perhaps there was a denial in concept that a wealthy Dublin merchant could feel equal to an Irish émigré of only moderate means or less than moderate means, and most certainly not equal to any one of those who had been evicted to witness their burning homes to which they could never return and so not worth consideration. Such a merchant, who would be mostly English in culture anyway if not by birth, would not have a reason to contribute. There's still a part of Dublin today referred to, perhaps a little contemptuously in some quarters, as 'English'. But the members of the Council could not understand why the emigrants wanted to leave England or Ireland or wanted to rise up with arms against the privilege of wealth in order to disrupt and change the established order. Alright for the wealthy to say that but there was a lot of soul searching in his speech. He queried the difference between classes and the enmity of nations and, perhaps being a little conscious and nervous of the recent and increasingly violent Chartist disturbances, he was querying the reasons that a subject of a country wanted to take up arms against its homeland. Noble in sentiment across the board perhaps, but ignorant of fact and the experience of being underprivileged and poor. It's an enduring cycle eager to repeat itself throughout histories. In 1848 Europe was imploding but, like a virus, it would naturally burn itself out eventually and stabilise somewhat until, of course, the next time. And there would be a few 'next times' in the coming decades and the Crimean War would be on its way shortly. In 1848 there was enough reason for many to want or even need to get away, and sadly, the selfish carelessness or excess risk of a single person, so it appears, on board the Ocean Monarch, added to the inherent lack of need to consider quite evident aspects of safety by those responsible for the ships, and had let all those people down.

There was established funding for the survivors of wrecks. In the smaller towns around the coast like Blackpool, there would be a 'whip round' in the inn for any of the quite regular shipwrecks where the unfortunate survivors who had lost absolutely everything apart from their own lives, were given the small but essential comforts of warmth, dry clothes, food, drink and cash and of course, humble accommodation. In 1912 when Blackpool had become a large enough town in its right however, a large concert was held in support of the Titanic fund, a shipwreck which took place far away from its shores but the sympathies of which were still relevant to the shore folk.

In 1848 in a large town like Liverpool with the richness of its trade and the organisation of its affairs, the procedures could be much more sophisticated and proved to be so. The Liverpool

Shipwreck and Humane Society was one such society. It awarded the Gold Medal of the Society to Thomas Littledale, Admiral Pascoe Grenfell, (the Brazilian Consul General), the Captain Lisboa of the steam frigate HBIM (ie Brazilian Imperial Navy) Dom Afonso, Mr Denham (Dane/Dani), master of the steamer Prince of Wales and Frederick Jerome, the 'courageous seaman' of the New World. The crew of Mr Littledales's yacht was also granted a sum of money. This gold medal was, 'Within one week voted, ordered and completed and the Times was enabled to bear testimony to the excellence of the work.' This was in stark contrast to the medals to be given out to those 'heroes' who had participated in the Peninsular War thirty five years since and who hadn't received their medals yet. In this case, it was proudly claimed that private enterprise exercised by the merchants and the 'gentlemen' of Liverpool had won hands down over the bureaucracy of elected Government.

A silver medal first class was awarded to each of the Commanders and four Lieutenants of the Dom Afonso, Commander Alcantara, lieutenants Torreao, Jose da Costa Lucia d'Aranjo and Tieve and Justino Jose, and to Jotham Bragdon the chief mate of the Ocean Monarch and Mr Batty chief mate of the Prince of Wales. A silver medal second class to the four seaman from the Dom Afonso (presumably who manned the boat). £15 (£1,215.17p) was awarded to five crewmen of the Ocean Monarch and the Prince of Wales and its chief mate Mr Batty was awarded £25 (£2,025.28p), to distribute among the crew. However, it is reported that the captain and crew of the Prince of Wales ultimately refused any remuneration for the cost of this generosity.

Both Frederick Jerome and Jotham Bragdon received the honorary bronze medal from insurers Lloyds of London, and Jotham Bragdon later expresses his gratitude, via the newspapers, to the people of Liverpool and all those connected with his involvement in the rescues from the ship and his honour in receiving the medals.

Frederick Jerome was presented with an additional £10 (£810.11p). He used his money well and financed his own magazine the following year, entitled, 'The World As It Moves' and though a resident of New York, set sail for California and, perhaps with dreams of golden nuggets, he'd given up the 'hard labour of the sea'.

Out of the royal bounty fund a sum of £100 (£8,101.13p) as a joint contribution by the Queen and Prince Albert for the relief of the survivors and was in addition to the £50 (£4,050.56p) awarded to Frederick Jerome for his Herculean efforts in saving many of the passengers. While the same necessities of relief with clothes and food and lodgings were afforded all the passengers there was also the matter of compensation. The ship itself was underwritten in Boston, Massachusetts and compensation sums for both personnel and materials would be referred to them.

The medals themselves were created by a Mr Wyon of Her Majesty's Mint and had a value of 16 guineas (£16.16s; approximately £1,500) each. As shown in the Illustrated London News October 18th 1848, the obverse is a sailor (with his pants on, and presumably inspired by Frederick Jerome) rescuing a drowning woman and child, which, in a male dominated world, was a little more evocative than rescuing a man and a child, and in the background is one of the little boats from the ships in the heroic mode of picking up survivors in far less than perfect sea conditions. The ship from which it had been despatched is in the background, and together, they represent the three major elements of the rescue. On the reverse is the Liver bird, emblem of Liverpool, encircled by oak leaves, emblematic of the self-sustaining belief in the oak timbers that first built the ships from the English forests and that had created the prefix of Great to Britain. Actually the best oak had proved to be swamp oak of Florida, since it had a proven greater resistance to cannon balls, a subject of jealousy and some conflict in former times between Britain and America. Timber ships would however be replaced quite soon by ironclad ships as demonstrated at the battle of Hampton Roads, Virginia during the American Civil war in 1862, and oak would continue in service as excellent structural timber and also make good household furniture.

Only four gold medals and twenty three silver ones had been awarded previously to those awarded for the action of the Ocean Monarch. On this occasion, five gold medals, seven first class and four second class medals were awarded by the Society, thus demonstrating the extent of the efforts, and the extremes of the human endeavour exercised during the rescue operation.

A chronometer, the size of a pocket watch, was 'Presented by the British Government to Capt. Joaquim Marques Lisboa, of the steam frigate Dom Afonso, of the Brazilian Imperial Navy, in testimony of their admiration of the gallantry and humanity displayed by him in rescuing many British subjects from the burning wreck of the ship Ocean Monarch, August 1848.'

Those passengers who were still wanting to get to the United States were given a free passage on the vessel Hope, which is possibly aptly named, and those that were too terrified or had no dreams to want to go anymore having lost all family and their dreams together, were given a full refund. Those who couldn't make the Hope could sail on the Sunbeam which was due to sail in a few days' time on the following Sunday. Many declined the offer of a voyage, despite it being free. Total passage money realised about £1300, (£105,314.64p) the fare for first cabin being £21, (£1,701.24p) the second cabin £12, (£972.14p) state room £5, (£405.06p) first deck steerage £4 (£324.05p) and the second deck £3.10s (£3.50; approx £284.00).

The passage money was accordingly returned by those acting on behalf of Messrs Enoch Train and Co of Boston, the ship's owners. The return costs home on this side of the Atlantic would be provided for, as would free passage for those who wanted to travel over the

Atlantic. All facilities such as bedding would be provided, and each passenger would receive an undisclosed sum on their arrival at Boston.

At a special meeting of the Committee of the Underwriters' Rooms, those prominent in the rescue viz; Admiral Grenfell, Thomas Littledale, and Captain Lisboa, were generously given the 'Freedom of the Rooms'. A tug boat of Messrs Baring Brothers and Co had been sent out by the underwriters to recover, with diving bells and other equipment, any portion of the wreck that was possible. The ship itself had been insured for £28,000 (nearly £3½m) and by 12th of October Messrs Baring Brothers were auctioning off from the salvaged ship, three and a half tons of copper sheathing, ten tons of steel, twenty tons of chain cabling, ten boxes of tin plates and one best bower anchor weighing 22 cwt (1.18 metric tonnes).

The owner and captain of the fishing boat that had picked up passengers from one of the boats was a William Syers of Seacombe and he had the distinction of being one of the last sailors now alive who had sailed with Lord Nelson. He was given a commendation at the inquest for his quiet part in the rescue which previously had gone unnoticed. He was an old sea dog by now and a seasoned mariner, and accepted as a 'worthy British seaman'. Also living in Seacombe at the time was a Francis Cofty, a coach painter by trade and another son of that other, worthy British seaman who had seen many years' service on the high seas during the Napoleonic wars. His father, Johann Cofty had been that worthy British seaman. He was Prussian, breathing the air and living off the land that is now Poland, and was pressed into service having been captured off a Dutch East India ship by the British navy. Service in the navy being the alternative to prison. He then comprised one hand of a multinational crew, such was the international diversity of the British navy. A year later, and not put off by the dangers of sea travel, Francis' elder, more materially minded and somewhat picaresque brother John, had left for America on the packet ship, the Guy Mannering in the July of 1849. In the October of the same year, the captain of the same ship had bemoaned the fact that the ship had to stay in quarantine in New York when, among seven hundred passengers, a large number had cholera and because of the cramped and poorly ventilated conditions, the disease was spreading among the healthy, and more were dying daily because the passengers were not allowed off the ship. There were already sixty patients lying ill with the disease in the Staten Island hospital in the city. Whether John Cofty jnr was worried enough to consider himself fortunate enough not to have travelled a year earlier on the Ocean Monarch or not, there were nevertheless thirty five natural deaths on this ship which from a total of several hundred was considered reasonable by some and inspired others to give the emigrant ships that moniker of 'coffin' ships.

The passengers of the Queen of the Ocean, having witnessed the events and whose emotions had been touched intimately by the distress of the rescued passengers transferred to them and the bravery of those involved in the rescue, collected £10 (£810.11p) of which £7 (£567.08p) was given to Frederick Jerome and the rest distributed to those of the crew of the ship's boat involved in assisting.

The Liverpool churches, filled with their Sunday congregations, gave generously to the fund for the assistance of the survivors. Those mentioned specifically are St Anne's at Stanley, £11.14s, (£947.89p) St Paul's Prince's Park, £56, (£4,536.63p) St John's £13, (£1,053.15p) and St Silas' £13. By 30th August the total of the fund had reached £1700 (£137,719.14p) and eventually exceeding £6,000 (£486,067.56p) as reported. The funding raised in Bangor and Port Penryhn for the survivors reached £54. 4s 10d (£54. 25p approx; £4,394.86p). Mr John Addison of Preston, a port itself further north up the coast, and he a barrister of the northern circuit, a man whom it seems was highly respected in his profession, collected subscriptions from his fellow professionals and the amount soon reached £150 (£12,151.69).

From Sheffield, probably inspired by the rescue of his townsfolk from the burning ship, came three boxes of steel razors to be presented to those three people most evident in the rescue, Thomas Littledale, Aspinall Tobin and Frederick Jerome. Their names were carved on the sides of the razors and inscribed, 'In Memory of the Ocean Monarch'. The donor was Mr Samuel Marshall, cutlery manufacturer of Eyre Street in the town.

Sketches of the dramatic scene were drawn for the drama itself, or to provide funding for the survivors through their sales. The sketch of the incident drawn by Prince de Joinville, in his own words, (J'ai fait de souvenir un petit croquis representant l'affreux accident, dont nous avons été temoins.) ('I have made from memory a little drawing representing the fearful accident of which we have been witnesses)' while aboard the Dom Afonso and was raffled off at his suggestion. The letter to Admiral Grenfell was originally written in French and perhaps, as a deposed heir to the French throne, in his recent exile in England he hadn't yet had time to become fluent in English, though his letter is quoted in English elsewhere, translated or otherwise. The sketch was displayed in the Exchange Rooms and to which there were four hundred and ninety one subscribers at 5s (25p; £20.25p) each, four hundred tickets being bought in the first two hours, the winner being a Mr Hulton of Hulton Park Bolton. This amount would equal £122.5s (£9,903.62p). Lithographic copies were produced by a Mr E Jones and presentation copies were presented to those who distinguished themselves most notably in the rescue operation, and all proceeds to go to the fund. One of the lithographic prints taken from this painting was sold to provide funds for the Sailors' Home. Other events took place in the theatres, and for some time afterwards the disaster was the subject matter of many a production in the smaller theatres around the country.

This was perhaps most notably demonstrated in Glasgow in mid-November of that year when a grand production of the 'Burning of the Ocean Monarch' at the Adelphi Theatre at the end of Saltmarket Street was in its rehearsal in the second act when a fire was noticed. The building was made entirely of wood and the insurers had refused to insure it because of similar, earlier incidents of wooden buildings burning down. Instead, the fire brigade concentrated on saving the adjoining buildings as a huge crowd gathered to watch, arriving on foot and in cartloads, and the more energetic and capable climbing the lamp standards in successful attempts to get a better view as depicted in a sketch of the event in the Illustrated London News November 25th 1848.

It was a busy theatre with a capacity of two thousand and a large cast who would lose all of their effects in the conflagration. It was estimated that about £10's (£810.11p) worth of property only would have been saved.

The fire was noticed when the actor playing the role of Captain Murdoch was admonishing his (imaginary) crew for setting the ship afire by smoking tobacco below decks. While this was not factually true, it added to the drama and emphasised the destructive nature of fire anywhere but, as he was pronouncing the words he noticed real flames in the upper gallery. An original reality programme perhaps. The theatre had only been built in 1844, and badly so, though it had been modified to the tune of £10,000 (£810,112.60p) recently.

Not so well patronised was the theatre in Chester in November where the shows were not well attended. At the Concert Hall in Nelson Street in a 'grand treat for the Christmas holidays', the Ship On Fire was part of a 'phantascope chromatrope' presentation, which is the more complex term for the popular magic lantern, in colour it seems. 6d (2½p; £2.25p) in the cheapest seats and half price for children. The burning of the ship still maintained an impact in the public imagination that the Titanic would have in future, public imaginations.

CONCERT HALL, LORD NELSON-STREET.

GRAND TREAT FOR THE CHRISTMAS HOLIDAYS.
ILLUSTRATED CONCERTS.

ON MONDAY, TUESDAY, WEDNESDAY, and FRIDAY EVENINGS next, the 1st, 2d, 3d, and 5th January, the SHIP ON FIRE and THE MANIAC, Illustrated by Dissolving Views and the Phantascope Chromatropes. The Ship on Fire forcibly presents to the eye the dreadful destruction of the Ocean Monarch, Burnt off Liverpool, August, 1848.

VOCALISTS.
MRS. W. COX,
MISS ANNE COX,
and
MR. FARQUHARSON SMITH.
Conductor, MR. F. SMITH

On Monday, the Maniac; on Tuesday, the Ship on Fire; on Wednesday, the sea Fight; on Friday, the Ship on Fire.

Body, 6d.; Gallery, 1s.; Reserved Seats, 1s. 6d.—Children Half-price. Doors open at Half-past Seven, to commence at Eight o'clock.

The Liverpool Mail Saturday, December 30 1848

The takings from an opera performance put on by eminent pianist Mr B Isaacs for 'his Friends, Pupils, Nobility, Gentry and Public of Liverpool' at the Theatre Royal in Williamson Square which also sadly wasn't that well attended but included the aria 'non piu mensa', which, in translation meaning 'no longer sad' might be true of those peaceful victims, now in death after their ordeal, but not so true of those who survived and who had lost everything but their lives. Nor is it true of Mr Murphy, the manager of the Killarney Savings Bank who had run off to America and was living well, it is assumed, with his misappropriated funds, for his wife and daughter, probably not complicit with his misdeeds and who were sailing out to meet him there, both perished in the disaster. It's not known whether he was eventually apprehended for his misdeeds but, unless he was an exceptionally insensitive person, he had paid a very high price for his crime.

ROYAL LIVER THEATRE, CHURCH-STREET.
SOLE LESSEE AND MANAGER, MR. JAMES ROGERS.

Revival of the celebrated Drama of
CLARISSE; OR, THE MERCHANT'S DAUGHTER.
The successful Drama of
THE SHIP ON FIRE; OR, THE LOSS OF THE OCEAN MONARCH, at Second Price.

ON MONDAY and TUESDAY next, the 20th and 21st instant, will be revived the admired Drama of
CLARISSE; OR, THE MERCHANT'S DAUGHTER.
Barbillon....Mr. H Widdicomb
Robert..Mr. J. Rogers | Clarisse..Mrs. J. Rogers
Dancing every Evening, by Melle. Fannie, Miss Dring, and Mr. Shaw
To conclude with the Drama of
THE SHIP ON FIRE; or, THE LOSS OF THE OCEAN MONARCH, which has been witnessed by 10 0 delighted spectators.
Tom Tackle..Mr. J. Rogers | Dick Dareall..Mr. J. Coleman

WEDNESDAY and THURSDAY, a variety of Entertainments. To conclude with THE SHIP ON FIRE.

FRIDAY, CURE FOR THE HEART ACHE, DAY AFTER THE FAIR, DANCING MAD, for the BENEFIT of Mr. H. WIDDICOMB, and his Last Appearance but One.

SATURDAY, a Favourite Drama. To conclude with the SHIP ON FIRE.

The Ship On Fire; The Loss Of The Ocean Monarch. Liverpool Mail November 18th 1848

At the drama production of, 'The Ship on Fire' or 'The Loss of the Ocean Monarch', at the Liver Theatre in Liverpool, there was criticism of the subject matter being rather macabre as the tragedy had not settled down in the minds of many. But the production was given good reviews and the house, especially in the cheaper seats, was full.

On the 6th of November Thomas Littledale was invited to a meal at the Royal Mersey Yacht Club rooms in Duke Street in his honour for his humanitarian efforts in the incident of the Ocean Monarch. 'In Honour of the Commodore', was spelt out on the walls in Marryat's flag codes, the codes used for the communication between the ships at sea. Even by 1912 by the time of the Titanic tragedy, electronic communication with Marconi equipment was relatively new and in its infancy and perhaps the innocent naivety of its use contributed thus to the extent of that disaster.

There were about seventy 'gentleman' of high social standing and included many of the participants in the rescue. Admiral Grenfell, Captain Lisboa, Captain Froes, and William Brown MP with a school and a street named after him eventually. Alderman John Bramley Moore was there as was Henry Melling, the secretary along with other Littledales, and his Councillor friends the Misters Tobin and Aspinall. Here he was presented with a silver and gold snuff box 4½ x 3½ inches (11.43 x 8.89 cms) long and engraved on the top with a burning ship. His family coat of arms is also included. Inside the lid is inscribed, 'Presented by the members of the Royal Mersey Yacht Club to their Commodore, Thomas Littledale Esq as a memorial of their admiration of the gallantry and humanity he displayed on board his yacht the Queen of the Ocean, in saving, under circumstances of great difficulty, the lives of thirty two of the crew and passengers of the emigrant ship Ocean Monarch of Boston, destroyed by fire in Abergele Bay on Thursday, the XXIV of August MDCCCXLVIII.' Or, Thursday 24th August 1848. Quite an essay for the engraver a Mr Mayer of Lord Street. Amidst the singing usually on tap on these occasions, there were the usual self-congratulations and many a toast to the legislature of the country, the royalty and the local politicians and the self-assurance that the class structure of the society to which they comfortably belonged would continue. Through the high sentiments of the need for the unity of those who came together to ignore national differences when often they were at loggerheads with each other, there seemed to be so many toasts that it seems hard to imagine that the eyes of many made careless by the drink would wander with a natural interest or lasciviousness to those many, and less privileged women who were no doubt waiting on, attentively and busily, the privileged gentlemen.

Life goes on and in the middle of September, Thomas Littledale had been competing in the Morecambe Cup for which there was a prize of £50 (£4,050.56p). He didn't win, and then the race of the following day had to be cancelled due to a lack of wind. But nevertheless one hundred and fifty 'gentlemen' sat down to a sumptuous meal in honour of Thomas Littledale and his 'humane exertions' during the dramatic rescue of the passengers of the Ocean Monarch. No doubt there were plenty of those gentlemen 'drinking' to that. Thomas Littledale and his friend George Aufrere would also be competing in their different vessels on Lake Windermere in June of the following year. George Anthony Aufrere Esq was one of the principal landowners in Bowness and lived in Burnside, a stone building, it seemed necessarily required to be reported.

By the end of September the yachting season was over and the vessels would be dismantled for the winter. In a grand 'sail past' in the Mersey, all the yachts of the club that had distinguished themselves by winning prizes in both England and Ireland during the year attended, but most of all this year would be remembered for the heroism displayed during the dramatic rescue of the passengers of the Ocean Monarch.

Another painting of the burning ship was created by Mr Samuel Walters and was raffled at the Exchange Rooms. Two hundred tickets were sold for 10s 6d (55p; £22.28p) each and it was won by a Mr Daniel Mather. Two paintings of the dramatic events of the year were displayed at the Manchester Free Trade Hall.

FREE TRADE HALL.

REVOLUTION IN FRANCE.—The Inhabitants of Manchester are respectfully informed that the EXHIBITION of the GRAND MODEL OF THE GREAT INSURRECTION OF PARIS, in June last, will commence on Thursday, November 2d, 1848. This Model comprises all the principal scenes and terrific efforts of the combatants on that memorable occasion.

These beautiful illustrations of the fearful insurrection will be accompanied with discharges of cannon, the burning of houses, the bombardment of the barricades, and scenes of military stations, &c.

In addition to the above will be exhibited, on a scale of unparalleled splendour and extent, MAGNIFICENT BLENDING VIEWS, each view occupying a space of 600 square feet, among which will be the calamitous destruction of the *Ocean Monarch*, from drawings by the Prince de Joinville.

Reserved seats, 1s.; gallery, 6d.; children half-price to reserved seats. Schools will be liberally treated with; for terms apply to Mr. Senior, Free Trade Hall.—To commence at eight o'clock.

The Manchester Courier November 1st 1848

THEATRE-ROYAL, WILLIAMSON-SQUARE.

FAREWELL BENEFIT OF MR. LLOYDS.

In addition to the
EXTRAORDINARY COMBINATION
of
AMATEUR TALENT,
assisted by
LADIES AND GENTLEMEN OF THE DRAMATIC
PROFESSION,
Mr. L. has the pleasure of announcing that he has been favoured
with the valuable aid of the celebrated Vocalist,
MISS EMILY GRANT,
who has kindly consented to appear in the character of Wilhelmina,
and introduce several of her most popular Songs.

ON MONDAY next, the 19th instant, will be performed Shakspere's Comedy of
TWELFTH NIGHT.
The principal Characters by the Gentlemen Amateurs who so ably performed the same Play for the Benefit of the Sufferers by the loss of the Ocean Monarch.
In the course of the Evening, favourite Songs by
MISS JESSIE HAMMOND.
After which, the Musical Farce of
THE WATERMAN.
The Characters by Gentlemen Amateurs and Miss Emily Grant.
To conclude with the Shakspereau Comedy of
TAMING THE SHREW.
The Characters by Gentlemen Amateurs and Ladies and Gentlemen of the Dramatic Profession.

The Liverpool Mail Saturday February 17 1849

The amateur performance of Twelfth Night at the Theatre Royal in Williamson Square in November of 1848 made around £150 (£18,258.95p) for the sufferers and which made more than £3,800 (£426,560) in total collected so far. The success of this play earned it a reprise at the Theatre Royal in February of the next year.

The officers of the Regiments (quoted 39th and 46th) based at the recently constructed and temporary camp at Everton, before a permanent military presence was established in the town, volunteered to give an amateur performance at the Amphitheatre. The title was topically and sympathetically entitled the 'Merry Monarch' and as well as receiving good reviews made over £100 (£12,172.63p), net for the survivors' fund. These same soldiers reprised their amateur theatrical talents later in December, this time in aid of the Northern Hospital, a place that had seen many of the injured sufferers in its wards.

After leaving for London the two princes, de Joinville and Duke D'Aumarle left a handsome amount towards the survival fund for the sufferers as the name by which the survivors were known. The Prince de Joinville left £10 (£810.11p) for Francisco da Salva and Joao Candido seamen on the rescue boats and Chevalier Lisboa sent £100 (£8,101.13p) to the crew of the Dom Afonso, and those who had distinguished themselves in the rescue, and named as Commander Alcantara, lieutenants Torreao, Jose da Costa Lucia d'Aranjo and Tieve and Justino Jose. But this amount was refused and instead forwarded to the relief fund for the survivors.

On the 5th May the following year, an oil painting entitled the 'Destruction of the Ship Ocean Monarch by Fire', was one of a whole host of prizes in a draw by the Art Union, at the Music Hall, Bold Street. Tickets were 1s 6d (7½p; £6.08p)) and various multiples above that. There were several prizes for winning, many of which for some reason, were stuffed birds. The painting itself measured 11 feet by 9 feet (approx. 3.3m by 2.7m), a large enough format to restrict the number of tickets sold to most private individuals, it might be imagined and not one for the living room of the common man or woman. Seven thousand lithographic copies, (at a production cost of less than a halfpenny (0.16p;) each for a contract worth £14 – (£1,704.17p) were ordered by a Mr Thom and it seems that the delay, and perhaps the disappointment in the quality of these prints, meant that the grand draw had to be postponed twice and it doesn't appear that ultimately, these prints were made available for sale.

In January 1849, while the memory of the burning of the Ocean Monarch had not faded, a pencil sketch and a print of the event was created by Mr Henry Melling, of Bootle in the town. He was an artist and the Honorary Secretary of the Royal Mersey Yacht Club and living in Hemer Terrace, Bootle Marsh, by the docks. He dedicated it to the club's Commodore, Thomas Littledale and it was considered far superior to the painting taken directly from the sketch of the Prince de Joinville. Perhaps this was because Henry Melling was from Liverpool and he wasn't French, but more likely that as an artist he would have had perhaps more skills and equipment, and certainly he could take his time in his studio. It was representative of an earlier phase of the destruction before the masts and rigging had collapsed, in fact about an hour earlier than the subject of other artists.

As a member of the yacht club he had been at the Beaumaris Regatta along with Thomas Littledale. His own yacht, the Gem, had been delayed in its departure because of a faulty anchor and so he missed out on the action and had been unable to be of assistance which he most probably would have been had he not been delayed. He eventually passed the Ocean Monarch at 6pm by which time it had been burnt to the water's edge. His own sketch consequently would have been subject to imagination and a little observation of other eye witness drawings or descriptions.

The painting and sketches of the burning of the Ocean Monarch, a topical and dramatic subject as much as the Titanic grips the imagination and maintains the interest today over a hundred years after its demise, changed hands as they came up for sale on the stalls of local fairs. That commissioned from the Dutch artist Herr Roosenboom (Nicolaas Johannes Roosenboom - transcribed as Rosenburg on one occasion) by the secretary of the British Museum, and measured 4' x 2', (1.2m x 60cms approx.) was sent by train from London in a crate to the Exchange Rooms at Liverpool for viewing and to be put up for raffle with tickets at 2s 6d (12½p; £10.13p)) each. It was won by a Mr English. The efforts and energies of Mr Warburton, Master of the Exchange Rooms, in organising the distribution of tickets won much praise.

Away from the theatres and the paintings there was a grand outdoor event held in Princes Park Toxteth for three days from

August 8th 1849. For this 'fancy' fair and exhibition, there were many contributions towards the largely charitable occasion organised in the absence of central or local government funding for the essential public necessities. Though it was largely a self-indulgent, self-promotional and self-congratulating occasion for both sponsors and patrons, it was a successful means of providing funds for those areas of society that otherwise would have had no funding at all. Most people would want to be seen contributing, maybe out of a natural compassion for humanity and maybe as a means to display their wealth, influence and power in the local and wider community. The Ocean Monarch tragedy featured in the motive for the fair. Three oil paintings including a large, 6' x 4' (approx. 1.8 x 1.2m) canvas of the burning of the Ocean Monarch were contributed by Messrs John Skillicorn and Co and were on view at the Town Hall prior to the their sale at the fair.

The fair was a grand event on a grand scale, and a central feature was that of the representation of a sailing ship constructed from the basic substructure of an existing a barn of 350 feet (106.68m) in length and with three tall masts up which chairs for 'ladies' and others could ascend to reap the reward of an aerial view of the park and proceedings.

Mr Lynn, of the Waterloo Hotel, a gentleman of the town and veteran of the Ocean Monarch disaster rescue while on board the Dom Afonso, seemed to have the monopoly of the catering for such grand occasions and he was likewise the caterer for this occasion. The Liverpool Standard of the 14th August 1849, in its review of the fair, thought it 'only right to mention that Mr Lynn's contribution consisted of 150 lbs of cakes, of various kinds, 120lbs of lobsters and 14lbs of anchovies for lobster sandwiches; 2 tons of ice; stock for jellies and fruit for the ice creams. He also furnished the knives and forks, table cloths, glass cloths, and the tea and table spoons; and made, during the week, using sugar and currants that were required which had been given by various tradesmen, 160 quarts of ice creams; 150 quarts of jellies; 60 gallons of punch; 3,400 buns; 10 large bun loaves; 200 gallons of lemonade; 100 sponge-cakes; and 50lbs of cakes of various kinds. In addition to the services of Mr and Mrs Lynn and the greater part of their establishment, they were assisted by several friends, who had offered their assistance for the occasion.' Even then the supplies ran out and the confectionary and bakers shops of the districts had to be scoured for resupply. Of course this mighty effort would have been assisted during the week's preparations by many a scullery maid and delivery man on his cart, working their worsted socks off. 120 lbs (pounds) translates to 54.43 kilos, 14 pounds to 6.35 kilos, 160 imperial quarts translates to 181.84 litres, 150 quarts to 170.47, 60 gallons to 272.76 litres, 200 gallons to 909.21 litres; 2 imperial tons translates to 2.03 metric tonnes, so not much difference with this last translation, all using the online conversion facilities.

Though the rain had spoiled the occasion for a couple of days, reducing the attendances and thus the takings to be made, Friday was put aside for the 'working classes', at least for those who could attend as cholera was sweeping through the overcrowded poorer areas of the city, and making demands on those of charitable leanings in their midst. The atmosphere of the fair was that of a carnival with stalls, in an immense marquee, that averaged takings of £100 (£1704.17) and occupied indefatigably by the ladies, which was ever their lot in life in the day, and led by the Mayoress.

On the large lake there were aquatic sports and boat races, and elsewhere there were side shows and alfresco exhibits of objects and of curiosities in tents. There was the electric telegraph, a galvanic battery and a camera obscura, marvels of their age. Magnificent floral displays and walks around the paths between the trees and the shrubberies were enjoyed by the refined members of society, numbering about fifteen hundred on the first day and constituting over £800 (£103,946.07p) in gate receipts, excluding pre-booked tickets, on the first two days. The total sum achieved from the fair exceeded £10,000 (£1,299,325.84). Exhibits of all kinds were on display and military bands provided the atmospheric music. In the evening, unfortunately when the rain came, the balloon flight of Mr Green was not as well attended, for two reasons, one being the rain and the other being that you could see the balloon rise from outside the park, without the need to pay an entrance fee. This was the bane of all organisers of balloon flights as their popularity increased with the progression of the century and the dream that man (and woman, and there were plenty of plucky and successful women who took up ballooning and parachuting) could actually fly. However the balloon ascent did take place successfully with Mr Green and his son and accompanied by paying gentlemen though one of these had to get out of the car since the balloon wouldn't lift the weight of four men. The second day too was spoilt by a late downpour. The horse drawn cabs and omnibuses that brought the throngs of people in all their finery to the Park took back an assortment of folk where, 'Fancy bonnets were woefully flattened; silks, satins, and muslins became dishcloths; and smart slippers became transformed into the resemblance of mud-be-smattered trenches on the feet of their owners.' When many of the tents and stalls fell victim to the destruction of the rain, the only construction that resisted the poor conditions was the large marquee put up professionally for the floral display. People rushed to the exits, 'Bonnets, hung flabbily down, like the feathers of a cock in a shower, and while the majority of young creatures left their flounces to flap about their ankles than expose their insteps, matrons more matured economically revealed those supporting fascinations which never before were indicated except by the charms of immaculate ankles.' The men must have got wet too but they weren't on display as much as the women were obliged to be, and perhaps the men wore socks so that their ankles would never be on display. Women would have to go through quite some pain and controversy before any kind of body exposure representing more than the ankles would become acceptable in the following decades. Today, much can hang out without inviting too much focussed attention, confined only perhaps to a few private jealousies or fascinations. When this well-covered throng reached the gates to call the cabs, which were in high demand, it brought the economic principle of supply and demand into the hands of another section of the socio-economics of society and the cab drivers charged a guinea (£85.06p) and occasionally five guineas (£425.30). There but for the grace of God. The political aspirations of the working classes change according to the opportunities that fortune offers to them and which itself creates the rise and fall of socialism, more so than the meagre skills of their political opposition.

On the Friday, in the stark division of rich and poor in the booming city, these 'working classes' were given entry, and included boat races, side shows and plenty of ale and buns. A repeat performance of Charles Green's balloon flight, a man that would spawn a family of balloonists that would itself encourage the interest in flight that would in sixty or so years, with a tweak or two in invention and the usurping of their dreams by the Wright brothers' heavier than machines, provide a rival to ocean travel, and create its own specific disasters in the process. When the people at the Fair saw the balloon rise they might have thought that they were looking at fools who thought that the human being could conquer the air but they were actually looking at the future and even the demise of the migrant ship and creating that future in its place for the annual transcontinental émigré or the annual holidaymaker from within their own kind. These working classes, representing many of who had drowned and lost everything, were not only those at the fair who drank up all the porter, ate up all the buns and used their fingers as forks and were the 'disagreeables' who mixed with the more wealthier classes, but who were nevertheless surprisingly, very well behaved and not subject to excesses. As reported in the Liverpool Standard of August 14th 1849 'we witnessed nothing of the character of excess, and no real and offensive forgetfulness, on the part of the humbler classes, of their proper position, and no presumption upon the immunity created by the occasion.' These were the likes of the people packed into the steerage classes of the migrant ships, hoping for the freedom of a better life, perhaps where they could aspire to the upper classes and look down upon the lower. Such is the potential penury of human nature. But the pickpockets had a successful day and a few young lads, who in the act of defending a fellow trouble maker, had a fight with the police.

On the lake in the middle of the Park, with a focus on safety at sea which was a topical subject in the public domain especially after the recent tragedy on Liverpool's maritime doorstep, there was a demonstration of a life-saving suit and apparatus which was a kind of life saving raft and which could keep five men afloat with provisions for five days. It was invented by a Mr Ryder of New York and had recently been brought over to Liverpool from that city by one of the ships and the 'fancy fair' provided a great opportunity to demonstrate it.

The conclusion to the fair consisted of a grand firework display and in all, in praise of the contemporary structure of society, it was claimed that in the three days that the one hundred or so ladies who had worked so hard in the cause of charity and peace and prosperity, had done more for human good than the three days of insurrection claimed for Liberty, Fraternity and Equality that the Paris revolution had claimed to achieve in its time. Though the jury would have to be eternally out on that claim, as through the ages, human society oohs and ahhs, and sways and falls, to the dictate of what it sees before it, from one extreme to the other, like the crowd at a football match, in its attempts to reach a natural balance of equality and fairness.

The simple lessons learnt from the Ocean Monarch regarding ocean travel were not applied in total to the Titanic and, in its social context, the human population of the earth will find its peace but become restless and engage in war once more such is the natural, if tragic, continuing evolution of the human being towards either its blissful omega point or towards it entire destruction.

But elsewhere, a painting wasn't enough to continue the drama or the sympathetic memory in some quarters. On the boating lake at Prince's Park, the activities were somewhat demure compared to the re-enactment of the tragedy at the Oddfellows third annual gala at the Botanical Gardens at Headingly in Leeds. The lake provided entertainments of various kinds which included Mr Wild's celebrated dog, Nelson, which had recently rescued a man from drowning in the river Ribble at Preston, a little north of Liverpool. Nelson would drive his master across the lake in a wash tub pulled by four geese, which is a spectacle somewhat curious to imagine, and perhaps somewhat unfair upon the geese, assuming these were not of a figurative nature.

A day of great spectacle and entertainment at this event concluded with a 'Grand Nautical Spectacle', 'representing the destruction of the "Ocean Monarch" by fire, together with the arrival of Littledale's yacht, and the noble exertions of the Prince de Joinville, the New World packet ship and the brave Frederick Jerome, effecting the rescue of the sufferers.' It was a disaster that had captured the public imagination on both sides of the Atlantic in a world that was committed to maritime transport in the absence of any other means yet of crossing the seas. The New World packet ship here gets an accolade unseen anywhere else. It had been the responsibility of the New York papers to bring forward the action of the New World which hadn't got much of a mention in the British papers at the time of the event. It was thought worthy of a mention that Captain Knight should be exonerated of any wrong doing as he was overlooked by the British press and authorities. The papers now also encouraged the Americans to honour Captain Knight likewise for his humanitarian efforts in putting out all his boats, and a crew that was willing to man them in difficult conditions.

As well as these spectacular events and theatre presentations, there was also the amenity to indulge the curiosity, pay a respect to bravery and death and make a profit by doing so on a trip around the wreck, and it was not just an excuse to take in the scenery of the Welsh Coast. The Ayrshire Lassie would leave Prince's pier at 11am and arrive back at 6pm having taken the route of the Ocean Monarch. Forward cabins were 2s (20p; £8.10p) and after cabins 1s 6d (15p; £6.08p)) with refreshments on board. The same happened to the stranding of the Mexico in the December of 1886 at Southport, a little further up the coast, a vessel leaving Liverpool for its transatlantic journey. Here it was not the ship or the crew that were the subject of the tragic loss of life, but rescuers that in quantity, drowned in the seas or eventually suffocated underneath their upturned lifeboats. Through a kind of morbid curiosity in there for some, there were trips arranged around this tragic vessel, too.

Mr Gough of the Woodside Hotel, gave the services of his omnibuses free of charge for anyone wishing to travel to Hoylake from Liverpool (and presumably this included the free ferry crossing too, unless provided from another source), to identify any of the several bodies that had washed ashore there, a direct line for the current or tides across the water from the Welsh coast at Abergele Bay, and from where the burning ship could have been spectacularly seen by the naked eye.

Later on the survivors, among them a woman who had gone through five pregnancies to have five children and lost them all, were gathered together by Messrs Harnden and Co at their offices on Waterloo Rd in Liverpool for the purposes of ascertaining their needs. A hundred and forty of the survivors had turned up and, even though they had been the recipients of charitable donations, they were nevertheless still bedraggled and in a sorry state. They were taken to the police station, when a public body like the police had a wider remit in the community, and were further furnished with more suitable clothing and effects which had 'been poured in with a liberal hand'. This arrangement had already provided the passengers as they were first landed with a number of topcoats and other items of clothing. It was here that those who didn't want to travel again but preferred to stay at home where it was relatively safer, received their money back which amounted to about £1300, (£105,314.64p) an amount which constitutes a large amount of fares.

One survivor, an orphaned, three year old child had little idea of what was going on. She touched the heartstrings of many an ordinarily sensitive human being including Queen Victoria herself who was making plans to adopt her. However, somewhat miraculously it might seem, the real guardians were found just in time. Less the Queen, but more those concerned with the status of monarchy, it might appear, had steered the idea away from royalty. It seems that the Queen would have never been allowed to adopt as the Constitution perhaps couldn't cope with a creature of unknown provenance, who may even have come from the depths of a troubled Ireland or one of the dirty, crowded and disease ridden tenements of industrial Lancashire or beyond to attain a place in the Royal household. No parents were located for the child, only 'guardians'.

The American Consul, Robert Armstrong, on behalf of his country, sent a letter of gratitude to the owners and crews of the ships involved in the rescue. The British Government Emigrant Commissioner was sent to Liverpool with £200 (£16,202.25p) to distribute among the sufferers and it was seen as a tragedy which affected all classes. And in this self-consciousness and focus on the city of Liverpool there was quoted in panegyric in the newspapers, using William Cowper's poem, 'Liverpool with all thy faults, we love thee still' but of course substituting the state for the city within the quote and talking generally about England, that a man resigned himself to love his country whether or not, and that this was relevant to the Liverpool of the day to do so.

£25 (£2,025.28p) from this Commissioner's fund of £200 was donated to the Northern Hospital in Liverpool for the medical attention received there for the victims of the disaster. Physical injuries appear relatively limited in numbers but mostly included severe contusions, broken limbs and burns. Some of the passengers were conveyed to the Birkenhead hospital across the estuary when, perhaps the Northern Hospital in Liverpool didn't have the capacity to cope fully. Some would be in hospital for over a month before being discharged with both physical and psychological injuries that would no doubt last a lifetime. It is not demonstrated how those with broken limbs, while on the ship might have managed to get off the boat, or not being able to jump, might have overcome their handicaps to reach the only very relative safety of the sea. Or how, not being able to jump at all but were confined and resigned to watch the flames that would eventually kill them, creep ever nearer to them, were actually taken off the ship and into the boats, by rescuers without medical skills and in disadvantageous circumstances. Those of course with broken limbs would have little chance of keeping afloat in the water and which would have reduced their chances of survival to the bare minimum.

Across the Ocean, on October 8th 1848, in New York's Castle Garden, before it became an immigration control centre, and when the tired and weary and often sick immigrant was at the mercy of all those who could unfairly profit from them as they naively disembarked, there was a Fair held in its grounds. Along with agricultural equipment and modern inventions including washing machines and dog power on an interminable turntable, there was a lifeboat claimed to be the very one that had been used by Frederick

Jerome to rescue so many people from the burning wreck of the Ocean Monarch. Even New Yorkers, it seemed, had forgotten the rest of the brave crews of the lifeboats and had put on a pedestal one of their own, unless it was the compiler of the report in the newspaper who exalted him through his own prejudice, deserving as Frederick Jerome was.

The money handed out to the unfortunate sufferers did not give solace to all, and the greed and selfishness of human nature is exposed when one of the recipients was taken to court in Leeds for not sharing out equally the amount given to the rest of the family of passengers. In a case of Neesom v Blaymire, the defendant had received £80 (£9,738.11) for all four of her (Mrs Blaymire's) party but only gave out a small portion of it (£5 - £608.63) to those entitled to it in the family group, keeping the rest for herself. In the subsequent court proceedings it was recommended that her property be confiscated and that she be confined to the House of Correction for forty days.

And of course, after any tragedy there are those would take advantage. If there were three hundred passengers affected by the loss of the ship, it increased the number of beggars several fold who would claim to have lost everything in the tragedy. If there were three hundred or so passengers then that number engendered four hundred or so beggars or more, all who had lost everything on the Ocean Monarch such is often the mendacious ruse of the mendicant without shame when opportunity strikes. Drunk and vagrant James Roberts, who was actually American, came begging at the shop of Mr J P Hirst, draper, at the New Market in Bury and claimed he was a survivor of the Ocean Monarch and begged for money. With the evidence of drink on his breath and in the suspect nature of his behaviour, the shopkeeper refused him assistance and had trouble ejecting him from his shop. James Roberts was later arrested and spent a month in the House of Correction in Salford. He was one of those potential hundreds who might take advantage of the tragedies of others.

THE PARLIAMENTRAY VERDICT

When the destruction of the ship was discussed in Parliament at Westminster, it was eventually concluded that it was more likely that the fire had been started by the stewards drawing off spirits in the store room, and this was corroborated by the reports of several survivors of a strong smell of spirits in and around that area. There were three stewards, two cooks and two stewardesses and all perished. That would also include one of the cooks who had jumped over the side with a barrel to keep him afloat till rescued, and it can be assumed that he sadly died at some time too, despite the report that he had been rescued, as the body of a 'coloured' man had been retrieved from the water. As these spirits would have been in the storeroom and one of the stewardesses lost her life in attempting to remove the stored gunpowder from the vicinity of the fire it was thought that a candle instead of a precautionary lamp was used. Everybody was quick to blame everyone else but the fire could not have started in the vent, when a passenger mistook it for a chimney, since this vent was blocked off by crates. It would be hard to understand that these crates filled with straw-to protect the contents of china within them, would not be considered as a hazard in a modern fire risk assessment and that consequently the ship would have been prevented from sailing. It was from the direction of the store room that the steward who was the first to inform the captain of a fire, emerged and hence the presumption that the fire had started there. It was regretted in Parliament that the crates had been stored as a bulkhead and which could be accessed easily by the passengers but less easily by the crew during the voyage. The smallest spark from the clandestine smoke of a pipe could have set off a fire in these circumstances. Indeed it was also regretted that a recent Passenger Bill passed through Parliament did not include a section dealing with the safer storage of combustible materials, and that these potentially dangerous materials should be boarded off so there could be no casual access, and that at least two seaman should be on board to act as safety inspectors for 'a spark from a lighted pipe falling amongst the straw of a crate would set fire to any ship.'

There was also the fact the American ship had just set off and was not long out of port. This fact and the fact that the American ships were 'notorious' for changing crews almost wholesale from one journey to another, meant that the ship's company had not yet had time to gel as a working unit and the one crew member did not know what the other might be doing and because of the differing nationalities, language might also be a problem. Even the Liverpool fireman on board of the Dom Afonso hadn't understood the original instructions from the captain to let the boats down to give assistance to the burning ship ahead of them because they were given in Portuguese, the mother language of the ship. The fireman on this ship, George Lee, was an English speaker, but this ship was only on a trial run without the responsibilities of over three hundred passengers and though the ship's complement was reduced in number, they were nevertheless an experienced and disciplined crew. George Lee was one of the men in the boat with Jotham Bragdon the mate of the Ocean Monarch for at least one of the rescue trips and who had all tirelessly rescued many people from the burning ship.

In all, the Parliamentary conclusion was that the captain could not have done much to prevent the complete destruction of the ship. There was no time to cut down all the masts to prevent injury and reduce the fuel for the fire which had taken hold fast and furiously and probably had a crew who were largely strangers to each other and communication and a pre-understood method of dealing with an emergency was not available to the captain. It was asserted, in answer to a question from across the benches at Westminster, that the Board of Trade had no power to order an official inquiry into the wreck as it was a foreign vessel, though this lack of powers was contested by the Opposition.

The conflict of language was a problem with the sinking of the Mary Rose three hundred years earlier in 1545 as it was found, in recent times, that the skeletal remains of the crew were largely Hispanic and thus might have constituted a language problem in giving instructions in English in the time of crisis. So some things don't, or can't, or are not allowed to change. Only a little more than forty years earlier that old seafarer once more describes his shipwreck survival from a man o' war, the Sceptre, in the British navy off Capetown. The crew was multinational and included many Americans impressed into service from ports in the West Indies. It was shortly after Independence in America, and there was no love lost between the British and American crew members, but by 1848 when the Ocean Monarch sailed from Boston, it can be assumed that a friendlier relationship between the two nations had evolved. The old seafarer was Prussian and ethnically German, himself pressed into service from a Dutch East Indiaman when Britain had to declare war on Holland due to its association with Napoleon. Such is the confused nature of nationality.

THE RECOVERY OF THE WRECK

The demise of the Ocean Monarch had created a gloom in those of sympathetic psyches in the town of Liverpool, and its memory was still strong in those who had to deal with its demise through all of the next year. The salvage had yet to be finalised and discussion about financial recompense yet to be completed. The valuable cargo of about £16,000 (£1,947,621.05 or £20,000; £2,434,526.32 in another report) consisted of about 700 (635.03 tonnes) tons of pig iron, sheet and bar iron, tin plates, steel bars, copper sheeting, earthenware and more. Some of the remains of the ship had been collected and towed into Liverpool by one of the steam tugs. They were left in the Prince's basin where they remained, presumably until insurance procedures were completed. Other bits were scattered about the northern shores as far as Cumberland (present Cumbria).

The ship had sunk in about 70 feet (21.34 meters) of water (at low water it was claimed that the wreck was about 30 feet - 9.14 meters - below the surface) and more than six miles from land and, soon after, the vessel can be described as 'split in the middle and is now covered in layers of deposited mud.' The wreck constituted a danger to shipping as it was in a direct line of vessels rounding Holyhead and for this reason it was located on the surface with a buoy but, for some time the bowsprit was occasionally visible above the water so it would have been evident to passing ships either as a curiosity or a reminder of the potential, but very real, dangers of sea travel.

Messrs Baring Brothers and Co, were the consignees in Liverpool and sent out a tug boat with diving bells and mechanism in an attempt to recover anything from the wreck for the insurance underwriters. The amount of the insurance claim from several reports is as much as $200,000 all in, of which $107,000 was insured. In Boston there were ten insurance offices in State Street underwriting the ship, cargo and freight in amounts of total $71,500 on cargo, $2000 on freight. Freight money is estimated at $13,000 'of which'$4,500 is insured'. When the ship sailed from Boston on October 15th the previous year, it had carried £60,000; worth of USA produce for Liverpool.

For the record, today's (2020) values read; $200,000; $4,152,095.24. $107,000; $2,221,370.95. $71,500; $1,484,374.05. $2000; $41,520.95. $13,000; $269,886.19. $4,500; $93,422.14. $60,000; ($1,965,658.23). On the 12th October, materials from the Ocean Monarch were sold off at the Broker's office in the Exchange Buildings, Liverpool on the same day and directly next door at No 13 where Thomas Littledale Brokers were selling off large consignments of South African and South American guano recently shipped in. The former with the figurative smell of tragic death for the sensitive mind to contemplate, and the latter the very real smell of discarded life for the nostrils to detect.

To be particular about figures and amounts, The Illustrated London News of September 30th 1848 describes the ship as being been insured in Boston in the offices of the Neptune for $3,500; the Hope, $5,000; the Suffolk, $10,000; the Franklin, $10,000; the Tremont, $11,000; the Equitable, $10,000, the Boylston, $8,000; the American, $10,000 and the New England $4,000. The cargo was insured at the Equitable for $3,000; the Boylston, $2,000; the New England, $7,500; the National, $5,000; the Lexington and the Kentucky Marine, $10,000 and $13,000 on the freight charges. The total of the insurance taken out on the ship, cargo and freight amounted to about $200,000 and the remainder of the sum, it was understood, was underwritten in New York. Using the inflation calculator, $1,000 in 1848 is equivalent to $33,111.65 as calculated for 2020.

THURSDAY.

On account of whom it may concern.

On THURSDAY next, the 18th instant, at Twelve o'clock, at the Brokers' Office, 14, Exchange-buildings,

150 Fathoms 1⅜ inch CHAIN CABLE,
2 ANCHORS, 35 cwt. each, and 1 ANCHOR, 18 cwt.,
Mooring CHAINS, Topsail SHEETS, BRACES, &c.; also,
About 10 Tons BAR, HOOP, and SHEET IRON,
„ 3 Tons SPRING STEEL,
30 Boxes TIN PLATES,
36 Sheets COPPER, &c.,

Recovered from the wreck of the Ocean Monarch, and to be seen at 23, Strand-street; likewise,

The HULL of the OCEAN MONARCH;
1300 tons;
(With whatever cargo may be therein;)

Which vessel took fire on her voyage to Boston, and now lies sunk off the Ormeshead. There is a considerable quantity of iron, hardware, &c. in her; and as the hull is but little sanded, with favourable weather diving may be pursued successfully.—Apply to Messrs. BARING BROTHERS and Co., Merchants, or to S. DUTTON and NEPHEW, Brokers.

The Liverpool Standard 16th October 1849

By the 16th October 1849, the salvage operators had already recovered much material to be sold off to defray the cost of salvage. The hulk itself, still with a viable quantity of material within it, was also offered for auction. And as more material was recovered, it continued to be auctioned off to ease the cost to the insurers.

On account of whom it may concern.

On Tuesday next, the 7th instant, at Twelve o'clock, at the Brokers' Sale Room, 14, Exchange-buildings,

DAMAGED MANUFACTURED GOODS.

100 Pieces Alpaca LUSTRES, LASTINGS, GINGHAMS, &c., ex Ocean Monarch, for Boston;
162 Pieces OSNABURGS, ex Mary, from Dundee.
Likewise,
13 Packages RETURNED GOODS, consisting of GINGHAMS, MUSLINS, &c.

The goods will be on show as above, and Catalogues ready on Monday next, the 6th instant.—Apply to Messrs. BARING BROTHERS and Co., and Messrs. GRAHAM, MACLEAN, and Co., Merchants, or to S. DUTTON and NEPHEW, Brokers.

Liverpool Mail November 4th 1848

On account of whom it may concern.
This Day, (Thursday) the 12th instant, at twelve o'clock, at the Brokers' office, 14, Exchange-buildings,
The MATERIALS of the OCEAN MONARCH,
lying at the Depôt, north end Prince's Dock,
consisting of Masts, Yards, Spars, Rigging, Chains, Anchors, &c. Two New Boats and Water Casks. The above picked up at sea, from the Ocean Monarch, for Boston.—Apply to Messrs. Baring Brothers and Co. Merchants, or to
S. DUTTON and NEPHEW,
Brokers to the Underwriters.

Liverpool Echo October 12th1848.

The recovery of the cargo was a difficult task and undertaken by the Steam Tug Company on behalf of the owners, Trains of Boston but this was abandoned until the ship was purchased by Mr William Blackey and partner of Liverpool. Presumably at some cost, they employed two teams of experienced divers who were working in teams of eight and the divers suited in what was described as a 'kind of submarine armour' made of waterproof fabric, lined with India-rubber. 'The dress (which comprises, as it were, boots, trousers and waistcoat, all in one piece) is drawn up round the neck, and a helmet or headpiece, of light copper, is placed over the head. At the front of the helmet are three holes fitted with glass, to enable the diver to see objects during the submarine excursions.' The helmet is attached to an India-rubber tube which itself is attached to an air pump worked from above the water and the foul air escapes through another tube. Weights carried on the back help the diver to descend through the water when their work would normally take about two hours but on these occasions had lasted up to three and a half hours.

In this way much of the cargo had been recovered and much had been put up for auction or sold by private contract. When all had been recovered, the wreck would be blown up by 'galvanic battery', which would seem by electrical impulse to the explosive used. It was advanced diving at the time and it was assumed, with some hopeful excitement, that these diving skills would be used in the future to retrieve vast, sunken treasures that to date had been irretrievable.

But there wasn't just the cargo and the materials within the structures of the ship that were recovered. At the end of September 1848, the steamboat working at the wreck recovered the body of man, who couldn't be identified because he was so badly decomposed and had virtually no face. He was about 5'8" (approx. 1.7m) in height and was wearing a black frock coat and pepper and salt trousers. There was no other means of identification on him. An inquest on the body was held at Liverpool where presumably he was buried, too.

Some of the cargo was salvaged quite soon after the ship had sunk and more recent, 21st century dives, reveal a scattering of plates at the shipwreck site. To those of us separated by a distance of time, it is just another migrant ship with a healthy payload of passengers in the romantic days of sail. To those people of the day it was the essential means of transport and travel upon which the whole economy of the world depended. To those travelling upon it, it was the escape to fresh hope and the accomplishment of dreams. The fire, a careless spark from somewhere unidentified, had let everyone down and destroyed the lives of many.

The figurehead, a full length Neptune, 7 feet (2.13 meters) in height, a colossal head with a gilded crown, slightly damaged, and severed from the body, representing Neptune, was probably one of the last parts of the ship to sink beneath the waves. Eventually it was washed up at South Shore, Blackpool though another report states it was washed up at Southport, which also states that a portion of the charred bowsprit was washed up at Nut End, when referring to Knott End opposite Fleetwood, further north still. Southport would have been confused with South Shore if at any stage in the instruction of the information was given verbally and wrongly transcribed accordingly. South Shore was a separate entity to

Blackpool at the time, with a different set of 'gentlemen' running it in their own interests. Southport is a little further up the coast from Liverpool but not as far north as South Shore or Blackpool and is a more fashionable resort today favoured by the high earnings of current footballers, some of who might topically one day be seen playing for Everton at the newly proposed Bramley Moore stadium in the city of Liverpool. The low tide at Southport stretches far out from the current coastline as it does at Blackpool but the nature of Blackpool's coastline meant that a high tide came right up to the building line and occasionally filled the cellars of those buildings on or close to the shore and as yet unprotected from a vigorous sea pushed relentlessly by a south westerly gale. So the lady from Halifax, who it is reported, found and took possession of the figurehead, whether or not she was holidaying in the coastal 'watering place' of Southport or the South Shore near Blackpool, must have been lucky enough to have been in the right place at the right time for a morning stroll near the receding tide, and with a little bit of providence or good luck on her side to come across the figurehead and understand its significance. Most reports have it correctly washed up at Blackpool where the sea brought its produce right up to the inadequately protected forefronts of the buildings and had a regular habit of flooding the town before the coastal defences were constructed for the first time a few years later, so she would have had less far to walk on the Blackpool beach, and indeed, she had watched it being tossed about near the water's edge before eventually being deposited upon the sandy beach, the gilt of its crown perhaps catching the morning sunlight and exciting dreams of richness generously deposited for free by the sea and without her having to risk the investment of a single penny in order to produce a profitable return. The report states that she claimed it for herself and carried it back to Halifax. Either she was a lady of some muscular strength to be able to carry it all the way home, or it was taken on a cart to the recently constructed and busy railway station in the town by friends or paid helpers who, it was deemed, were not important enough to mention. Back in her home town of Halifax, it was displayed for a while in the shop of a Mr Mercer, a plumber and glazier of Russell Street. But by 1907, its location was unknown in Blackpool as a letter to the newspaper was enquiring about its whereabouts as the correspondent claims that a witness had seen it carried from the beach and that 'it was painted white and adorned with a golden coronet, not a full crown.'

Parts of the wreck continued to be washed ashore and those that could be identified as being from the Ocean Monarch, as the Morecambe correspondent reports about those bits that found themselves in the bay there, were quickly picked up and turned into memorials of the tragedy, and sold on for high prices. And there were those who would take advantage no doubt and create a memorial out of nothing and sell it on, like the mediaeval selling of indulgences, which might have created a true Christian cross of about a mile long and as proportionately wide if all parts were able to be collected and pieced together and St Joseph's revered last, bottled, breath which could perhaps fill a hot air balloon. Such does selfish opportunism negate a sense of morality within the human being.

THE DOM AFONSO (POSTSCRIPT)

The Dom Afonso, as it would be officially known, was anchored in the Sloyne in the Mersey on the 7th September in a more celebratory mood as it was the anniversary of the declaration of Brazilian independence from Portugal in 1822. It was bedecked with flags, and the merchants of the town were invited to lunch on board. Life goes on, but the tragedy of the Ocean Monarch would no doubt have had a significant place in the conversation. It was a Liverpool built steam ship and, in the words of captain Marques Lisboa, 'a beautiful sea boat which goes well under canvas.' Despite its hiccups at the beginning of its life as a sea going vessel it was in Brazil the following year to assist in the fight against the popular rebellion there. Captain Lisboa's French sailing friends on board the Dom Afonso on their trip to Dublin the year previously, would have understood the threat to their status in their exile from their homeland. In South America many men from the Dom Afonso were lost in the eventual fighting that was to take place there. Here, the status quo was maintained, the Imperialists won and, in the victory, the economic gap between rich and poor continued to be. The rebel leader, Joaquim Nunes Machado, who did not favour violence but was drawn inevitably into it and killed in the action could, perhaps, have been the Che Guevara of his day. Change is often a negligible quantity.

As well as somehow saving the Portuguese man o' war, Vasco da Gama, from shipwreck during the conflict, Captain Lisboa also, in another interesting incident, while stationed off Rio de Janeiro during a storm and in the dark, a boat overturned evident by the cry of its capsized occupants. The boat contained two 'negroes', a different species of human being in the mindset of the day, and a concept continuing today in the endemic qualities of the suspicions and self-assertions in the interactivities of all human beings even of the same race and ethnic status. Captain Lisboa jumped into an acquired and beaten old canoe and braved the seas in an attempt to rescue them. Whether he was aware that they were 'negroes' or not, is not known, but they were still human cries and not cries belonging to that perceived different species of living creature, just like the cries of a perceived underclass of human being came to his ears during the rescue operation for the Ocean Monarch. He was a man of the sea and a guardian of all those who sailed upon it. The action could be seen from the torchlights of the shore and he was given a great cheer in his successful rescue during which he himself had to dive into the sea and swim for some distance. Perhaps he was also conscious in memory of the bravery exercised by that lower class people who were not a different species either, during the demise of the Ocean Monarch only the year earlier, and was accordingly inspired to act.

The Dom Afonso itself didn't have a very long life, running aground and subsequently wrecked in 1853 at Cabo Frio (Rio de Janeiro State and north of Rio itself) while chasing slave ships (recently a hundred and ten Africans ready to be landed as slaves had been seized, liberated, and given daily paid jobs) when South America appeared to be a Continent where slave trading, in the exercise of the sugar trade mostly for Europe when near one million were forcibly transported from Africa, was still an option preceding the violent eruption in North America in the next decade.

MIGRANT SHIP SAFETY

There had been advances in medicine and safety before the destruction of the Ocean Monarch, but not all were popular enough to be introduced into the area of public safety. Probably since they all had a financial element, an investment of which couldn't be returned from the outlay of capital, and commitment to each for the common good would not be conducive to financial profitability. However, whenever there was a tragedy like the Ocean Monarch, the collective conscience was pricked and whether through guilt of past tragedies or concern for future safeties, many a newspaper's editorial desk would be full of suggestions, some of which would be useful enough to pursue in discussion until eventually time stretches to a distance from the event at the end of which all becomes irrelevant and can be forgotten and everything can calm down, and the suggestions could be ignored as there is no pressure to produce an explanation or an answer.

The Liverpool Mercury of October 1848 claimed that an investment as small as £100 (£8,101.13p) could have probably saved the majority, if not all, of the lives on board that tragic vessel. Thirty years before, the paper had discussed the proposals of a Mr Egerton Smith who had devised plans and published a booklet on ship safety, but it was regretted that this pamphlet, if indeed there was an existing copy at the time of writing, had been ignored and would by now be completely unknown. And from that time other sensible suggestions had been forwarded to the paper for exposure and publication but none would ever be taken up seriously. The paper blamed the fact that it would take investment of money to create safety measures and claimed that it should be the ship owners' responsibility to invest. The introduction of the newly devised life buoys could be provided for an additional rate of 5% on the cost of a fare so it wouldn't eat much into the profitability of the ship owners' returns, nor make any small increase in the fares they might consider necessary, unattractive to potential travellers. A reference was made to Ayckbourn's 'invisible' life preserver and swimming belt which would take up no more room than a shirt when worn on the body. Four hundred of these life buoys at an estimated cost of 5s (25; £20.25) each on the Ocean Monarch could have saved the lives of four hundred people. These people, the newspaper it can be assumed, had the ability to jump into the sea from where they could be saved, but however they arrived in the sea they could survive, unless in the most extreme of circumstances, long enough to be rescued.

Since the tragedy of the Ocean Monarch, many more suggestions had come to the editorial desks. It was suggested also that those steerage passengers who were 'too poor' to afford a mattress of their own, and who brought loose straw on board with them should be provided with a stiff, cheap, tick cloth to cover the straw, as straw was a highly inflammable material. It was also pointed out that on a naval man o' war or troop ship, (though the men o' war at least, being almost permanently at sea could become very leaky themselves, and couldn't always be presented as a paragon of safety; that old seafarer once more sailing from Capetown to Montevideo to take on the Spanish there, writes of his ship, the Elisabeth being leaky and it had to be constantly bailed out) describes the fact that there are two men who had the responsibility of fire watching, systematically in short periods of time, of inspecting the ship and making sure that the discipline involved in fire control is maintained among the ship's company, and each watch is reported to the captain. If this discipline was conducted on a migrant ship, where the responsibilities of smoking and the use of matches or candles on board often made essential in the darkness of the holds where the steerage accommodation was contained, was less understood, then there would be much less risk of the creation of a careless spark to cause the destruction and loss of life as recently witnessed.

Another correspondent to the newspaper was a Mr J P Joule, later to be celebrated as John Prescott Joule, the electricity practitioner who would eventually create Joule's Law, and who developed the use of electrical motors to replace the steam driven motors at his brewery in Salford. He suggested that the methods used by the crew to put out the fire, honest enough in execution were, however, counterproductive and actually beneficial to the spread of the fire by not cutting off the air supply. He suggested that the act of throwing the water into that environment (and in sufficient quantities) created a draught and increased the circulation of the air and actually fed the fire more than starving it.

Various methods of fire control were suggested and basic fire extinguishing facilities should be placed around a vessel according to the size of the ship. A compound of potash and sulphate of iron made into a paste and, when needed, a sufficient amount placed into a bucket of water would help to control the fire and reduce the amount of smoke, which was the greater of the serial killers more than the flames themselves. The idea was to contain the fire to give passengers and crew sufficient time to evacuate the ship. Also when ships needed to carry a small quantity of gunpowder, it should be kept in a fire proof container as that developed and marketed by Milner and Sons. It could be pointed out that the knowledge of gunpowder on a ship would help to panic the passenger for, in the case of a fire emergency, they would be expecting the ship to blow up at any moment and there would be no hope of rescue. There would have been no explosion on board the Ocean Monarch, at least until the last person had left the ship, had the powder been stored in such a container.

Mr Henry Howells of Bristol who had travelled across to America as a cabin passenger on a packet ship which included about a hundred and twenty steerage passengers, presented his experience to the newspapers. He wasn't surprised that the Ocean Monarch alone had been destroyed by fire but more surprised that, in his experience, many more ships had not succumbed to the same fate. He refers to the fact that there was only a single water closet on the vessel he had travelled on recently and that was up on deck so, when the hatches had to be shut down during adverse weather conditions, and the steerage passengers confined to their quarters for days on end that, without reference to any popular toilet humour, the stench was unimaginable within those confines.

Also smoking was rife and even after 'lights out' about 9pm smoking was carried on. Pipes and cigars were quickly hidden under pillows or mattresses if it was suspected that an inspection might take place. There is also the problem that some of the passengers were dirty, and even verminous, before they came on board and perhaps they should be medically checked or cleaned before they boarded. On the occasion that Henry Howells reached Sandyhook in New Jersey, the vessel he was in narrowly missed the obligatory quarantine when disease is reported or even suspected. Drunkenness was also a problem as cheap liquor could be obtained from the captain. As a steerage passenger, reaching a port, having lived for weeks under such conditions, would be equivalent to reaching paradise, whatever the landfall of arrival.

There were continuing improvements in medicine, and chloroform was one of them, which would become available to a ship's surgeon. John Simpson a Scotsman, had devised the use of chloroform in 1847 and it had begun to be widely practised the previous year but not entirely accepted until it was used on Queen Victoria herself for the birth of her eighth child some six years or so later, (before that the pain of childbirth might be considered natural, especially by the male, and perhaps shouldn't be interfered with, a fact that might be accepted in remote principle but considered as unnecessary and, in every safe way, should most definitely be interfered with, by the female).

On the 25th June 1845 a man named Phillips demonstrated his invention of the 'fire annihilator' which was the precursor of the modern fire extinguisher, though not patented until some years later and too late for the Ocean Monarch and other ships and properties damaged or destroyed by flames. It was estimated that fire was responsible for £2m (£243,452,631.58p) worth of damage and about a thousand deaths annually in England alone. In an understanding of the causes of fires, that oxygen, heat and fuel were the three main ingredients as the requirements for fire to thrive, his 'annihilator' then, 'consists of a small vessel containing the gases known to be non-supporters of combustion; namely carbonic acid gas and nitrogen, which gases are in a quiescent state until brought into action by touching a small trigger at the top of the vessel.' As a portable vessel this annihilator would successfully put out fires especially when water was not readily available. Ironic perhaps when considered on a ship which was surrounded by water but, in the words of the Ancient Mariner, not a drop to spare or, more importantly, plenty to spare but not a drop that was easily accessible. And also, the right concoction of chemical compounds thrown down between the decks could have converted the smoke into harmless vapours so it is claimed.

Life saving equipment was available but was perhaps too young a concept to be fully taken on in a commercial environment or adapted to the laws of safety. While the floating qualities of cork were put forward as a life saver, if properly distributed throughout a ship, then it was regretted by the manufacturers of Ayckbourn's life saving, inflatable float which could be worn within the clothing, and that was 'as portable as a handkerchief'', that it hadn't yet been adopted or accepted. It only weighed six ounces (170 grams) and being ready in a moment was also not liable to burst. In an advert in the newspaper shortly after the disaster, it was regretted that these had not been available to be used on the Ocean Monarch. In a sense of irony, the manufacturers, Frederick Ayckbourn of London had tested these out in the Thames. By the Chain pier at Chelsea a young chap called Coombs cooked a dinner in the river by a floating table while wearing the belt. He was in the water for over an hour and was watched by over three thousand people. It clearly worked. The dramatic loss of the ship and the tragedy of the passengers encouraged debate on the safety of ships and the construction of fire-fighting methods and chemicals. Ships had lightning conductors so there was no moral reason not to invest in fire-fighting equipment.

There was also a demonstration of life saving equipment at the Wenlock baths City Road London in May of 1849 when the manufacturing process had been tweaked to a successful outcome. It was attended by several men with an interest in life saving at sea, including those representing the Russian navy who weren't slow to put in an order to supply their two steamship frigates being fitted out at Blackwall (ships and equipment which could be used against Britain in a few years' time during the Crimean War).

The successful demonstrations focussed on the use of cork, as tragedies like the Ocean Monarch had demonstrated that, even during an active rescue, many lives were lost because drowning was imminent as few could keep afloat in the water long enough to be rescued even though rescue was at hand. It was shown that a sailor's bedding rolled up into the regulation bundle of 11 inches (approx. 28cms) and weighing 9lbs (9 pounds; approx. 4 kilos) could, when rolled out keep three men floating and a bolster, the pillow, to rest the head upon, and buckled to fit around the waist, could keep a single person afloat. Any common and portable item in the sailor's or traveller's, natural baggage could be stuffed with shredded cork and used as a float in case of emergencies. On the Ocean Monarch Captain Murdoch had had to use the initiative of the moment to arrange the preparation of enough floats for the vast majority of his ship's company and human payload by laboriously and painstakingly chopping down the spars and the masts when time was clearly not on his side, his actions nevertheless saving many lives.

Various other experiments with cork mattresses and cork equipment to store in a lifeboat in case of capsize were conducted. Considerations were even given to bullocks and, (for some not readily available reason, camels), to demonstrate that even livestock could be saved, it would be hoped perhaps, for the benefit of the animals themselves rather than the profitability or the convenience of food, that transporting animals represents. A similar experiment had been given at the Royal Clarence Baths in Plymouth where a raft made up of lashed planks and covered with a cork mattress was floated on the Tamar to Saltash and back by a crew of several men.

The demonstration of the rubber life saving raft at the Prince's Park in Toxteth preceded those feats of Paul Boyton, the Irish American, whose demonstrations and feats attracted large crowds thirty years hence. While Paul Boyton used a rubber floating suit and an oar to float himself across the English Channel (before Captain Webb had completed the feat unaided), the use of cork was being developed in the cause of safety on ships and always the Ocean Monarch was given as an example, and the more recent example of the Caleb Grimshaw, of how many lives could have been saved if the floating qualities of cork could have been used. In the beginning, the problem was not in the principle but in the practice of manufacture where in 1848, the machinery could not cope with the volume of production for the particular needs of large ships, especially the migrant ships. It was suggested that in the steerage accommodation the mattresses of the beds and other furniture could be constructed with a cork fibre content which would be a means of floating, and used as jackets. Despite successful experiments having already taken place, the enthusiasm for production stalled at the difficulties in the means of production. Cork as a life jacket was already in use, as the promoters of Ayckbourn's life saving equipment maintained.

As far as lifeboats were concerned a ship carrying three hundred passengers with only four boats was a disaster if anything untoward would have happened and on the Ocean Monarch, it did. Even that vessel was fortunate to be near the coast and the port and in touch of passing vessels which might or might not be willing or able to lend their hands.

There were however, life preservers on board, but only it seemed for the use of cabin passengers and no instruction seems to have been in place to inform the passengers of the right action to take in case of emergency. J K Fellowes had one which may have been provided with the ship or he may have bought it privately, since he was a seasoned traveller and would have known the risks. It seems then that the steerage passengers, if regarded as the lowest class of human individuals, could be assumed to be considered as mere cargo. There was no-one to stand and demonstrate the use of life saving equipment nor indicate means of escape like you would get on a modern passenger aeroplane. Thomas Henry, a merchant and another cabin passenger first heard the alarm of fire but thought nothing of it at first. But when the reality was soon evident he put on a life preserver, inflated it and lowered himself down on a rope into the water. Not a strong swimmer he owed his life to the inflatable preserver and, he claims, Providence too. He was later picked up and was alive and well to indicate this at the inquest. He had sailed with Captain Murdoch before and had no reason to doubt his abilities. Perhaps Thomas Henry, a regular traveller it could be understood, had purchased his life preserver privately and it might even have been an Ayckbourn. Another passenger in the second cabin did not have a life preserver but jumped into the sea at the same time, when there was no other evident option and trusted in his own sense of Providence that he could somehow survive. It is not known whether he did or did not. India rubber was in its infancy when later demonstrated at Princes Park in Liverpool, but was increasing in popularity and the city of Brooklyn, from where it appears that this knowledge was brought over to England. In contemplating fire safety, the city was in favour of constructing a Bucket Company and this company would be provided with fifty buckets as well as 2000 feet (over 609 metres) of rubber hose in protecting the city against fire damage.

But, while the transport of emigrants was a profitable business, often more profitable than the cargo the ships carried, the safety of the passenger was not paramount and, as the mantra of modern safety considerations throughout industry resounds, 'safety rules are written in blood' and meaning that many people have to suffer injury or die before a rule can be considered necessary.

The Caleb Grimshaw was a ship sailing from Liverpool later in the November of 1849 and also caught fire and the emigrants bound for America suffered terribly during the days that they were afloat in the burning ship, subject to the rough treatment of the captain and crew and the accepted and divisive and social distance between the English and Irish on board. With the echoes of the Ocean Monarch still resounding in the ears, it brought out disdain for the emigrant ships that didn't even carry a lifeboat or an adequate means of putting out fires. Where emigrants could be considered as disposable cargo it was further demonstrated on October 4th 1848. Captain Mcfee and the crew of the schooner Ann from Liverpool had a rough time in the Gulf of St Lawrence on their way to Quebec and, with the fear of sinking in the storm, the hatches were closed and fastened down to prevent the unnecessary ingress of water, and thus securely trapping the immigrant passengers within the vessel and leaving them to their fate. For all the captain knew or cared, it was a certain death for those trapped. However, a passing vessel, the Princess Ann, a higher perceived status of the same name, fortuitously passing perhaps when the storm had abated somewhat, was able to rescue the passengers when the crew and captain were nowhere to be seen, no doubt rowing furiously to the safety of the nearest landfall of terra firma.

And with the same considerations, in December of the same year, a vessel, the Londonderry, carrying a hundred and fifty hopeful emigrants to their potential Atlantic staging post at Liverpool from Sligo, Ireland ran into difficulties in a storm on its way around the north of the Island. The steerage passengers were ordered below off the decks where they most commonly congregated on these journeys because that's where the fresh air was. They were locked in the inadequate space of the steerage accommodation which measured a mere eighteen feet by a maximum of twelve (approximately 5½m x 3½m) and about 7 feet (approx. 2m) in height where at least seventy of them suffocated because there was no ventilation or provision of air. A greater ratio of cattle survived than human beings. Most of these steerage passengers were described as poor farmers from the Sligo and Ballina areas of the North of Ireland, refugees from poverty and the potential of starvation and eviction, whichever came first. Locked into a compartment resembling a modern ship's cargo container, one man managed somehow to break out through the covering at the top and sought out the first mate who went down to investigate. Unlocking the doors, the air was so foul that it put out the flame in the lantern and, when a second lantern was brought, it put that out too. The procedure then was to uncover the tarpaulin which secured the top of the compartment from the ingress of sea water from the waves which broke over the ship, and rendered it further airtight. The light then revealed a heap of dying and dead bodies, which, according to the Sun newspaper, 'There lay, in heaps, the living, the dying, and the dead, one frightful mass of mangled agony and death – a spectacle enough to appeal to the stoutest heart. Men, women and children were huddled together, blackened with suffocation, distorted by convulsions, bruised and bleeding from the desperate struggle for existence which preceded the moment when exhausted nature resigned the strife.' When the boat put into port at Derry, soldiers were sent to prevent anyone leaving the ship as the rumours of dead bodies on board were investigated for truth. It was then that the true horrors were revealed on investigation by the magistrates, as the piled up bodies were removed. The desperate story of survival was told as the marks of hobnailed boots were evident on many of the bodies and the flesh was scratched and bleeding as there was a writhing mass of humanity in the fear of death and the struggle for life. Many children were orphaned. Three of a family of nine survived without their parents or their other siblings.

Captain Johnstone, the first mate and the second mate were convicted of manslaughter which doesn't appear to have been a capital offence at the time, but only just not. The crew were criticised for their careless part in the affair and steam companies were advised to pay better attention to steerage passengers and not just to consider them a convenient cargo to be landed at Liverpool as discarded poor and useless tenants to the landowners of Ireland. It was also claimed, but not proven, that many of the bodies had been robbed of what little value they possessed. The bodies were stored in a warehouse before investigation, identification and burial could commence, and the living were conducted to the town hall to receive assistance.

So, in some cases, the lessons of such a dramatically memorable tragedy as the Ocean Monarch had not been learnt and the difference in class between the steerage passengers and the captain and cabin passengers persisted. But those steerage passengers on the ship were at least travelling voluntarily as opposed to those paupers from the workhouses who were systematically transported to Australia from Ireland. Earlier in September about forty young girls between the ages of fourteen and eighteen were given passage to Australia. Considered useless to their own society they were handed over as easy prey to the captain and crew of a ship that might want to treat them as their right, as the female convicts of the convict transport ships from England were reportedly treated. Such is the temptation of the predator when there is deemed no redress for its actions.

Poverty in Ireland, which provided a driving motivation for emigration or violence against its oppressors, is demonstrated in a newspaper article of July of 1848 when the much travelled correspondent of the London Illustrated News took a trip to Killarney in Ireland, travelling by train from Dublin to Mallow and taking a coach from there along the forty two miles to his destination. He speaks of houses, cottages, huts and wigwams (or mud hovels), this latter predominating all along the roadside deserted by the occupants either evicted, forced into the workhouses which had been largely helped by the Irish Poor Laws the previous year, or annihilated by the potato famine. But, where the Ocean Monarch was concerned, it was not only the impoverished and destitute, the numerous beggars among which crowded around the transport that stopped in their village or town as the much travelled correspondent describes, 'I imagined I had seen squalor, that I knew the face of wretchedness, that I had looked upon misery and destitution, and knew their lineaments; but I can declare most solemnly, that all the previous squalor, filth, wretchedness, and poverty that I ever beheld – even in the lowest lanes of London, the filthiest wynds of Glasgow, or the most hideous closes of the old town of Edinburgh – were cleanliness, gentility and comfort, compared with what I saw.'

But it was also the more well to do who could not pay for their more extensive abodes, as the large and over-substantial farmhouse as seen by the same correspondent was 'equal in architectural appearance to the most comfortable farm-houses of England'. But of this Irish one, its windows were broken and its walls were tumbling and the ground around it was overgrown with weeds and was reclaiming itself as bog land. The tenant of this property had been on the Ocean Monarch. He'd absconded because he couldn't pay the rent. Only a man was mentioned. Perhaps he had a family as well. And, as the writer is informed, he perished on the ship. A cruel price to pay for being unable to pay his rent.

The merchants of Liverpool themselves had raised more than £2,000 (£243,452.63) for the sufferers of the Ocean Monarch and the scepticism between the Irish and the English in the city is born out in this statement from the Liverpool Mail. 'We copy the following testimonial to Liverpool generosity and appeal to the better feelings of Irish residents who may have been misled by truculent and unprincipled incendiaries'.... 'We hope that such beneficent conduct will have its due weight with the Irish labourer in Liverpool, and that by sobriety and peaceable demeanour, he will prove himself no unworthy object for the exercise of kindness.' A sentiment which might sound like a quiet threat where, in other words, it might imply that the Irish labourer should be glad to accept his lowly place in society, be nice to the landlord or he might just get thrown out of his house.

Two families that would intermix with the family of the old, shipwrecked mariner left Ireland about this time. Some would become labourers in Liverpool amid the stark conflict of differences between the two aspects of Christianity in the city, Protestant and Catholic. One line from Wexford with an aural tradition which reflects involvement in the 1798 rebellion and previously subjected to confiscation of lands and executions, and the other from Mayo, decimated by sixty per cent of its population during the time of the continuing Great Hunger and the emigration resulting from the same. They came to Liverpool, in which there was a large Irish population, occasionally having to change a name in order to get a job.

Somewhat ironically later in the year, a steamer named the Prince of Wales which plied between Fleetwood and Belfast was in collision with another vessel sailing from Liverpool, a sloop, the Jane and Jessy. While off the Isle of Man, this sloop ran into the side of it, causing a large hole through which the seas rushed in. The captain was able to run the vessel aground near the Point of Ayr (Isle of Man) but three lives were lost including two passengers who were cattle salesman and who ignored the advice of the mate to stay up on deck, instead retiring below decks to retrieve their clothes and money, and lost their lives in doing so.

Also with the name Ocean Monarch and remarkably in the same year, an incident is recorded on that ship from Le Havre to Quebec of two 'respectable' looking women, a middle aged mother and her adult daughter travelling steerage. The captain was curious as to why such a pair of posh looking women should be travelling steerage and gave them, with some prejudice it could be imagined, more attention than the others. He found out that their passage hadn't been paid until a 'gentleman' appeared on board on arrival at their destination with their passage money. They were then revealed as wealthy people found to be the widow and daughter of Jacques Lafitte the former French banker and royalist. She was also the daughter in law of Marshall Bertrand, close friend and companion of Napoleon. Somewhat noble sentiment streaked with guilt is given to them as for once in their lives they had to endure, 'the worst of all situations – the steerage of a ship during a long voyage. It is at least a comfort to know that they have been befriended on their arrival, and it is to be hoped they will yet enjoy the comfort and tranquillity to which they have won the right, by privation and suffering.' Not really a way to promote the berths available on the ships to the excited emigrants hoping for a new life away from the continuing 'hardships and sufferings', of their natural lives and who had steerage as their only option and who would not be greeted by friends and comforts on their arrival, their only true companion being their strength of will to survive.

Sometimes safety as a consideration on these ships only kicked in after the event. Survival, in some cases, might have to depend upon the closeness to the shore, not to a pre-arranged and practised safety structure enforceable by law. When the old seafarer reached the shore at Capetown after clinging on to a floating timber for an eternity and his legs almost too weak to carry him out of the surf and onto the solid ground of the beach, he had been lucky. If out on the open sea, then safety depended upon the willingness of some to risk their lives to save others, without any pre-arranged plan. Blackpool where the body of Alice Wrigley was deposited by the dispassionate sea is a town largely renowned for its entertainment, but it has fulfilled other roles, mostly in war times as a refuge to the nation. It is a coastal town and the coastline to the north and south of it in the Fylde is littered with shipwrecks, blown there by the fierce south westerly winds onto the unseen and insidious sandbanks and recorded from the 18th century and onwards. Its littoral dwellers have always been used to finding bodies washed up on its shores and showing great compassion to those that survived, often rescued by feats of human bravery and selflessness. And it is true of all shore dwellers. At Ramsgate just two months after the tragedy of the Ocean Monarch two emigrant ships bound from Germany to America, were stranded on the sandbanks of the Goodwin and Long Sands. The reports are a bit confusing as two are factually different. The first ship, the Burgundy, was noticed by a Liverpool schooner on its way to Holland and all the passengers and crew were taken off in such numbers as to be in danger of overwhelming the little vessel. Several fishing smacks bore down from Deal and Ramsgate and it seems that the passengers were transferred to these and were landed at Harwich. In true Dunkirk manner, about two hundred people were rescued. Once on land these desperate German emigrants were treated in such a humanitarian fashion that the newspaper could, 'confidently say the case of the Burgundy is not even surpassed by that of the Ocean Monarch'. Clothes, warmth food and shelter were immediately on hand and even door to door collections for donations were undertaken and generously responded to. By morning, the wreck of another vessel, the Atlantic, was found as it was beginning to lodge deeper in the sands with no hope of freeing itself again. Out again from the two ports, Ramsgate and Deal, came the luggers and other vessels. Several of the crew had already been lost but the rest of the crew and passengers were all brought off safely with skill and determination in difficult seas. In March of 1849 there was another shipwreck, that of the Floridian, an American ship sailing from Antwerp for New York, on the Long Sands in which all passengers were lost.

FREDERICK JEROME

Frederick Jerome was a crew member of the New World sailing as mate in 1848. He was a native of Southsea, England, probably born in Moscow Buildings to a father William and mother Frances, on 14th May 1824 where, in his very first breath, he would have taken in the salty sea air. There are different reports of how he came to live in America. One account is that he joined the navy at a young age and, finding the life somewhat unsuitable, jumped ship while in England and engaged on a merchant vessel which was bound across the Atlantic. This is less likely it would seem as he would be wanted man, like Joshua Penny, an impressed American citizen, who jumped ship from the Sceptre while at Capetown and lived rough on Table Mountain for a while. It was the ship on which that old mariner was employed as a quarter gunner, and Joshua's capital crime was only naturally quashed when the same ship was wrecked and so consequently he did not belong to a ship any more. The papers report, rightly or wrongly, that Frederick had moved with his family when he was just a young child but, however he got there, he had settled in New York and by 1838, was sailing the seven seas at a young age, it would seem. He had been nearly eight years in the American merchant service before obtaining his registry in Liverpool and by 1846 he was an experienced seaman 'before the mast'. He first came of note in seafaring circles when he showed he was not afraid, through bravery and a loyalty to his profession as a seaman, to swim through cold, perilous seas, in order to rescue both the ship, the Henry Clay, upon which he was employed, and the many helpless passengers and crew within its timbers.

By 1846 he was an able bodied seaman on the Henry Clay, a ship named after a Senator who never got to be president despite trying, and defeated in nomination by the same James K Polk who, in 1812, was also responsible for the war with the British, taking a little trip down to New Orleans where, in that era, they got the British 'runnin' as the patriotic song goes.

It was on the Henry Clay in the March of that in 1846 Frederick Jerome, an Englishman still perhaps with a traceable southern English accent that saved the lives of the seven hundred passengers on board by his heroic deeds. Caught in a severe gale off the New Jersey coast, the ship was driven onto the notorious rocks of Barnegat, and stuck fast there in danger of eventually breaking up. Those gathered on the coast could do nothing apart from watch the tragedy unfold just like those helpless observers on the Welsh coast who in couple of years' time would see the burning inferno of the Ocean Monarch. The boats, had been washed away but would have been useless anyway in the severe sea conditions. Up jumps Frederick Jerome, a twenty three year old able bodied seaman who had already been 'before the mast' for several years. With the strength of his youth it took him, so the report states, over two hours to swim to the shore with a line from the ship. Sometimes being lost from sight below, and then gratefully appearing above the waves, from watchers both on the ship and on the shore, he reached terra firma in an exhausted state, where the shore folk rushed into the water to drag his almost senseless body onshore before the tide could take him back. But he had brought with him a lifeline, a hawser wrapped around his shoulders and which had cut painfully into his body. With this line attached to the ship all the passengers were saved though it must have taken time, patience, and courage with anxiety to get all safely to the shore in the difficult conditions and all done by the shore folk, fishermen and families of fishermen who knew and respected the sea and all those who travelled upon it. Probably Frederick was recovering with a warm drink for much of the time, but it would seem unlikely that he would rest for long. A passenger on board the ship, and evidently a very rich one, seeing a very probable death before him and having a desire to live a little bit longer it seems, offered a reported $100,000 ($3,276,097.05) reward for anybody who could save his life. Because all the passengers were saved, it would include this gentleman, but it is not recorded that Frederick ever received his reward, deserved as it was. Had he received the $100,000 of the frantic offer from the chap who was reluctant to part with his money, then perhaps Frederick might have considered changing his profession and many lives on the Ocean Monarch two years later would have been lost by his absence. Such is life dictated by the unpredictable fluidity of circumstance.

After his heroics during the disaster of the Ocean Monarch, he had become well respected in America where he lived in New York at 343 Water Street. In England after the rescue, the Prince de Joinville had shaken him warmly by the hand, and had given him several gold coins. When the New World had docked at New York at the end of its voyage with its heroic crew, he was given the freedom of the city, presented in a gold box during a grand ceremony on 29th September at the Mariners church with such a large congregation that there were many left outside. One of the ladies rescued from the ship was on the stand. This 'lady', it could be assumed, would be one of the cabin passengers rather than one of the steerage passengers as she warrants the title of 'lady' and had probably arrived on one of the later ships on a passage provided by the insurance.

'Mr Jerome', the newspaper informs, 'has sailed out of New York these past seven years, has married in the last two and has since had a child. He is a poor man and has nothing to depend upon but his hard earned wages as foremast hand when on the deep.' But poor men can be brave as much as they can be intelligent or intellectual, and his heroics were to be further commended and rewarded later, and in England would reach as high as Queen Victoria herself. And, despite the somewhat patronising tone of the newspaper report, he also became a rich man.

Not only was he given the freedom of the city of New York but also that of Liverpool, too. Here, the mayor, Thomas Barry Horsfall, in a special meeting of the city council, tendered the freedom of the city as well as a gold medal and the generous thanks of the Council. In Boston the inscription on the Humane Society medal awarded there read, "Humane Society of Boston to Frederick Jerome, mariner ship New World, who by his gallant conduct was instrumental in rescuing the crew and passengers of the ship Ocean Monarch, burned at sea August 24 1848."

As well as his recorded heroics in the wrecks of both the Henry Clay and the Ocean Monarch, it appears that Frederick was a kind of serial life saver, the exact opposite of a serial life taker, that serial killer who perhaps yearns for all the publicity and the lasting memory of its misdeeds. The San Francisco Call in 1895 claims he had rescued over a thousand lives in his lifetime. While he was involved in the saving of this amount of lives, those hundreds from the Ocean Monarch were the result of a joint effort by many brave men (and brave women too, if their stories could be told), so cannot be ascribed to Frederick alone. He also saved the lives of the Captain of the Lucky Star and his family who were wrecked on the coast of Formosa (Taiwan) in 1862, though no detail of this incident has been found. Locally known in San Francisco as the 'Commodore', his life saving propensities were known to have saved many lives in the Bay of San Francisco as he worked as a boatman in its waters there.

F. Jerome, a Hero of the Sea.

San Francisco Call 16 August 1895

In 1895 he was living at 1402 Polk Street in San Francisco, a street named after the President of the USA, of Liberal politics, involved in the Mexican war of 1848 and land acquisition, including that with vestigial British interests, while Frederick was saving lives from the Ocean Monarch.

While in New York in 1850 he lived in Ward 16 with his three year old son Patrick and his Irish wife Bridget. Patrick, it is made evident later, appears not to have survived. Frederick is also listed in the 1851/2 New York directory and whose occupation is a mariner living at 72 Oliver in the city. Though maintaining this New York address, perhaps leaving his wife and child there, he had made the move to California in 1849, where he became a true '49 er', leaving New York for good some time later with the fruits of his generous rewards. He sailed on the ship Tarolinto and probably in a state room cabin and never had to tack the ship to steer it in the right direction according to the dictate of the wind. And probably drank wine at the captain's table. On the ship among other 'gentlemen' was a Mr W S O'Brien, an Irishman who had made good through capitalism and left over twelve million dollars on his death in 1876, and who by 1848 was already a rich man owning mines in Virginia before discovering a rich vein of gold in California. Though he would be a lifelong friend of Frederick, there is no mention of him sharing the wealth of his friend. Frederick himself was a wealthy man and had initially gone in search of gold with his friend, but he ultimately preferred to work as a boatman on the Bay in San Francisco, and continued to save lives from the dangers of the sea. It was in his blood it would seem, and there was no way of extracting it from him. While a boatman in the Bay, one of his most noted and successful rescues was recorded when he saved the crew and a passengers of the British ship Wiscasset with a cargo of wheat for England and which was driven onto the shore in a severe gale. Frederick Jerome was the right man to have around at the time and accordingly went to the ship's assistance. Though the details are not well recorded, he nevertheless succeeded in difficult conditions to rescue the crew of thirty through the crashing surf.

After the short time of gold digging, if that was his initial incentive to reach California in the first place, and also establishing his own periodical magazine, he became embroiled in the contortions of the bloody and vicious Civil War, on the side of the Union. On his ship, the Alabama, he was captured by the Confederate frigate, the privateer Florida, and taken prisoner on board, but the formation of a plot to escape and take over the ship which was ascribed to him was discovered through a breach of confidence in one of the men. As the ringleader he was manacled and chained to a gun in double irons (or other reports claim he was chained to a mast) for two days and then handed over to another ship as soon as he could be. It seems that, in the same account, he was then transported to Japan where, through great good fortune and coincidence, once there, he was recognised by an ex crew mate and so was able to make his way back to his homeland. In all, this separation both in war and peace, his poor wife Bridget had to cope with the isolation and lack of knowledge of where he was or whether he was alive or dead. An eventual homecoming might have been of the magnitude of the coming together of mother and child in the Northern hospital of Liverpool all those years ago after his heroics during the tragedy of the Ocean Monarch. It would be gratifying to consider just that, as a romantic re-union but maybe he had had left his socks out of place before he had left and there was reason for Bridget to remain infuriated until she could have it out with him on his return, perhaps after the initial kiss. Such is the trust in relationship in the expression of relief. But Frederick probably hadn't left his socks out at all and he would have, is to be expected, been welcomed equally the open arms of a true compatriot in the often stormy voyage of the life of any human being on being reunited once more.

By 1870 Frederick is living in San Francisco with Bridget where he is merely described as a boatman. His house value is stated as $4000 ($79,534.05) and personal cash of $150 ($2,982.53). So a large enough house in which to keep his socks tidy.

When visiting New York in 1881 as a 'gray headed old man' he was given every courtesy by the Maritime Exchange as his fame had not dwindled. Memories of the 29th of September 1848 where he was given his gold box and the freedom of the city presented by Mayor Havemeyer at the Mariner's church were still apparent.

In 1894 he had travelled back over to England and, along with his wife, no doubt within a comfortable cabin, was wined and dined both by the Prince of Wales, the future king Edward VII in the yacht, Osborne, and by Queen Victoria at her Osborne House residence on the Isle of Wight.

As Captain Frederick Jerome, the end of his life arrived on August 3rd of 1900. He had in fact already been declared dead in the Halifax (UK) Guardian of March 1852 which includes in a brief, inserted statement, 'Jerome, the sailor who distinguished himself at the burning of the Ocean Monarch, was recently killed in an affray in Central America.' The source of the information is not known but evidently the news desk of the publication had been somehow misinformed. However, at the time of his real death, he was buried at the Oddfellows Cemetery a few days later where the funeral was conducted by the California Society of Pioneers in San Francisco, the Pioneers being those who arrived in California before 1850, and to which Frederick had been voted in as a life member. He had requested a simple funeral which was duly delivered by the Pioneers at the Pioneers' Hall. A masonic band provided the music. He left in his will, his whole estate of $20,000 ($620,176.19) to his wife Bridget and after her death his property would go to nephews and nieces in England, since it appears that his only son Patrick, had not survived. It is not known whether these relations in England were ever located and duly received the bequests. He also left a gold snuff box, a gold medal, and a gold bear to the society.

But to the rest of the world a single, short obituary distributed to the press merely declared him to be 'an old time sailor who had the credit of saving over a thousand lives.' Time moves on and it was now fifty two years since his most notable heroics connected with the Ocean Monarch. The San Francisco Call in reporting the probate referred to him as a 'prominent pioneer' with no mention of the renown of his rescues at sea.

But even as early as 1851 at the Wolverhampton grand annual steeplechase in England there was a horse called Frederick Jerome so his name, since there doesn't appear to be that name before in the records, appears to have been quickly absorbed into the popular imagination, if perhaps largely forgotten in the passing of time to the present day.

JOTHAM BRAGDON

Jotham Bragdon and Frederick Jerome have been singled out as the two main characters in the rescue operation. Both are pretty much forgotten about today but, while Frederick is recorded as taking advantage of the recompense of his heroic deeds and leaving a genealogical trace in the records, Jotham more slips into obscurity and, though there is evidence that he too settled into some reasonable material comforts from his deserved recompense, his genealogical footprint is very light and less easy to follow.

From his name printed so frequently in the newspapers of 1848, Jotham Bragdon is probably the master mariner on the 1860 census for Newton, Hancock Maine, age 47 and living with his Irish wife Julia, son Irving and daughter Margaret. 1848 was the year his son Irving was born though it is not certain whether his father had become a hero by the time of his birth or not, but his wife Julia would have got hold of the news of the Liverpool tragedy, perhaps not knowing initially whether her husband was alive or dead as the news was unloaded from the first packet ships to arrive in Boston after the event with an incomplete story. The many Bragdons of New England are mostly farmers or mariners and the families probably interconnected through marriage. In 1860 Jotham had a real estate value of $1200 ($37,358) and personal funds of $200 ($6,276) so probably quite reasonably well off. In the New York Directories there is a Jotham Bragdon, seaman, for the years 1864 to 1867. His name was forgotten long before that of Frederick Jerome and he seems to have slipped quietly into obscurity as the records conceal his name among many others of the same name for the casual observer. His son Irving married in 1883 but the census records show an Irving Bragdon in the Bloomingdale Asylum at White Plains in New York by 1900. Though this Irving maybe a relative other than his son, Bloomingdale, as the first hospital for the 'mentally insane', is named after the road upon which it was established in 1821, a road now called Broadway and never had there been a drama acted out on Broadway as that cruel reality show represented by the tragedy of the Ocean Monarch in which among the whole varied contingent of humanity, villains were found out and heroes discovered, tears of sadness flowed, the warmth of human compassion poured forth in a fountain of abundance and the joy of reunion was experienced at an unimaginable heart-bursting level.

Before leaving Liverpool, where he had been brought aboard the Dom Afonso in September of 1848, he wrote a letter of gratitude for publication, which is transcribed thus; 'Being about to leave Liverpool I take this opportunity to express my deep sense of gratitude to the inhabitants of Liverpool and its vicinity, also to the captains and officers of several ships in port for their unbounded kindness to me since my escape from the ill-fated ship Ocean Monarch. While on board the steam-frigate Affonso I received every attention; and on my arrival on shore the hand of friendship was offered by all; not the hand alone but my friends contributed to my every want, which enables me to leave Liverpool in far more comfortable circumstances than I had hoped; - a kindness I can never forget and for which I shall feel under the greatest of obligations as long as my life is spared. May God bless them, as man never can, be he ever so wealthy and liberal. I would also acknowledge the receipt of a medal from the Liverpool Shipwreck and Humane Society, as an expression of their opinion of my conduct during that trying scene, and also to encourage me and others to do what is really our duty, that is, to save life and relieve suffering whenever it is in our power, for which they have my sincere thanks, and may God bless them in their labour of love while on earth they live (but may a like scene never come before again), and, when done with time, may they receive their reward in that bright world above, where shipwreck and suffering never enter; which is the humble prayer of Jotham

Bragdon, late chief mate of the Ocean Monarch. Liverpool, Sept 10th 1848' (Liverpool Albion).

His script is accused of being uneducated by the Spectator newspaper when it printed the letter in its pages. His vernacular on the ships with his peers might not be expected to be as educated as a journalist in a newspaper, but suited to the occasion of his daily routine, and his letter to the paper has possibly been assisted by another more educated hand, one that was more used to words and never had to scale the rigging or tack the sails constantly on the open seas. But in eloquent language and sentiment the correspondent of the Spectator accepts that language is not the perfect gauge of education but the action of human sentiment speaks louder than the most erudite of scripts. In praise of Jotham Bragdon, while withholding reservations, we can be mostly complicit with the sentiment of the paper (quoted from the Spectator in the Nottingham Advertiser of September 22nd 1848) thus; 'This week the papers publish a letter which is curious in the way which the writer helplessly struggles to express very creditable feelings in language ludicrously enfeebled by the rudeness of unpractised composition; and we should all be apt to say, in excuse, that the writer is an "uneducated man". It is Mr Jotham Bragdon, the mate of the Ocean Monarch, who distinguished himself in directing and aiding the efforts to save the passengers. On that occasion, when helpless mortality was contending against the combined elements of wind, water and fire, and its own terrible infirmity, panic, he restored courage to the affrighted by his cool presence of mind; his arms, trained in hardy service, overcame the waves, and served for the lives of many besides his own; his practised eye and hand gave him mastery over the sailor's instruments, even in that scene of chaos; his manly heart was literally tried in the fire; but allowing the utmost for a noble nature to start with, an immense proportion of all this was the result of education. And the most admirable part of the spectacle, in our estimation, is not the mere saving of life, but the display of perfect self-devotion to the dictates of social piety.'

Perhaps education is only essential in a complex technological society, but if a person only needs to tend the crops and dig the potatoes then the acquired knowledge and high skills necessary are learnt as naturally as a spoken language is, from those teachers who have learnt from those who have gone before them and who have naturally learned without a stroke of homework.

ALICE WRIGLEY

So, back to Alice Wrigley. Though from the industrial area of Lancashire where much of her family were in the cloth trade she was, nevertheless, well to do and able to indulge in the relative luxuries that a cabin passenger could expect. On board, she could sit comfortably in a room with space and read a book. Those in the steerage only had their three tiered bunks as well as providing their own straw bedding for the comfort of the sixteen day journey across the Herring Pond that the Atlantic was casually referred to. She had something to lose as well as her life. For those who had very little or almost less than nothing, they may well have come off materially better after the event though perhaps in a meaningless way.

She is not mentioned on the published passenger lists and she must probably then be one the 'four others' appended to the list and travelling as cabin passengers and who are not mentioned by name or maybe the clerk through carelessness or disinterest had not written down her name. Perhaps she, or her party, was a late arrival. Her husband it is reported in a single newspaper article some time later, had moved over to America the year previously and she would have then been one of the many who was going out to join relatives over there. She was twenty six years old and, if that name which appears in the parish records refers to her, then she originated from Bury where she had married at nineteen years old as a minor and she herself at her marriage is described as a gentlewoman from Tottington, though her last address, as a married woman is given as Bolton. Whether she was travelling alone or whether she was in the company of the three other unnamed passengers will probably remain unknown. There is no record found for any children from her marriage.

Once she had boarded the Ocean Monarch, she would probably have had just enough time to witness an introduction to the company and the society of the other passengers, perhaps even sat in relative comfort to read a book, which she could never have finished, and perhaps enjoyed an evening's conversation at the dinner table the evening before sailing if she had had the time and not been rushing on to the ship at the last moment. However, she would not have had time to become too well acquainted with the other passengers before that excitement, curiosity or apprehension when meeting strangers for the first time and with whom there should be a close association for a couple of weeks, either favourably or unfavourably, turned to the worst fears of the human being, that of the confrontation with death and the belief that there could be imminently little or no chance of escape from it.

The body of Alice Wrigley was identified quite quickly after being found despite being washed ashore many miles to the north. She was buried soon after recovery and was only originally identified by her sister through her clothes drying out on a hedge in the churchyard at Bispham. When her sister arrived at the church with her supportive companion from her lodgings, she recognised her sister's clothing and immediately exclaimed with a deep sadness, when maybe her heart had sunk into her stomach, 'Oh I know my sister is here. There are her clothes on the hedge.' Her clothes were there among the clothes of the others as the only means of identifying the disfigured or mutilated bodies of the shipwrecked victims. There was time after the event for her to compose her own funerary verse for the inscription before the monumental mason was given his remit. The records of the Wrigley, and of her pre-married name of Haslam, families, are a bit vague in their early dates to positively identify Alice's family in name, but her husband and father both shared the same name of James and both worked in the same cloth industry as bleachers.

James Wrigley who, it seems, had only travelled the previous year, would have been expecting Alice to join him in the September of 1848. He had worked as a bleacher in the cloth industry in Bury and while in America he is described as an engineer, a career he continued after the loss of his wife. He moved on, as is natural, and married Jeanette Sutherland from Scotland in June of the following year and settled in Lancaster a town to the east and outside of Boston, then moving to Clinton by 1860 where he continued to work in the cloth trade.

THE INSCRIPTION ON ALICE WRIGLEY'S GRAVESTONE

Beneath this stone a sister lies,
The briny waves have closed her eyes;
Unthinking at the morning light
To sleep in death's cold arms at night.
The strong must yield to death's strong grasp,
But Jesus died, and rose, and reigns,
He will raise her sleeping dust to life,
And bind the tyrant Death in chains.

In Memory
of
ALICE
Wife of James Wrigley, aged 26 years,
late of Bury.
She perished at sea, in the endeavour to escape from
the Wreck of the ship Ocean Monarch,
when on fire,
26th of August, 1848.

The flattened headstone, to the south west side of the All Hallows Church in Bispham, Blackpool. Picture by Barbara Reed

Of those bodies washed ashore along with Alice Wrigley, the ages range from ninety two years to seven months and disregard the stillborn child, such is life independently allotted to each human individual.

At the end of the first page of the parish records, the last two records belong to the victims of the Ocean Monarch and the first inclusion is that of Alice Wrigley, from Bolton, 'one of the passengers of the Ocean Monarch' and buried on September 9th. Then below the insertion for Alice Wrigley; 'Three women cast upon this shore. From their appearance evidently having formed a part of the crew and passengers of the Ocean Monarch an American ship. Age unknown.' These burials were conducted on the previous day, the 8th so presumably there was no hope of identification of these unfortunates as there was in the case of Alice when it was possible to wait a day longer.

The margin is copiously scripted and reads; 'The splendid American Ship Ocean Monarch of 1300 tons burden left the Mersey early in the morning of the 20th August with about 360 persons on board including the crew and emigrants and when only a short distance from Liverpool (inserted; between the Ormeshead and Abergele) was literally destroyed by fire and as near as can be calculated 170 persons met with a watery grave many of whom but a few hours before were buoyed up by ....(illegible then continued on the next page with the same difficulty in reading)... ?high hopes of the future.'

Over the page for the same date of September 9th are recorded, 'Four women and one man of whom one was a girl about 17 years of age. Evidently having formed a part of the crew or passengers of the same vessel belonging to Trains Line of Boston packets.' And, in the final column, 'Ages unknown'. A very busy couple of days for the Rev Pearson of the Church in which the frail and often unpredictable mortality of the human being was evident for all.

As far as the Ocean Monarch goes, the human being is still prone to tragedy and calamity, in which dreams are crushed and hopes upturned, villains triumph and where good deeds go unnoticed and selfishness rules, but where a moment of human self-sacrifice, of extreme bravery and selflessness, can give a belief in the future of humanity if, indeed, it could be believed on this congested earth, that it has a future at all.

PASSENGER LISTS

These lists are taken from the British Newspaper archive and accessed via Findmypast.

The Manchester Examiner printed a list of the known survivors by 26th August and those saved altogether include the 32 by the Queen of the Ocean, 160 by the Alfonso, 6 on the

fishing smack and 17 on the Prince of Wales, leaving 173 unaccounted for.

This evidently incomplete list of the passengers, recorded as having been saved, when first published includes;

Elisha Bannister, B D Elisabeth and W (it is not made clear how these are identified), James, Mary and Edwin Booker, Jeremiah Brenihan, Jane and Thomas Bruttal, John, Leah, Henry and Frederick Brown, J Bristow, Mary Brittain, Doris and Eliza Burns, Ellen Callaghan, Ann and Abby Callaghan, Joanna and Margaret Carney, Mary Cashman, Denis Carling, James Cooper, Thomas Constantine, Denis Corcoran, Peter Cox, Edward and Ellen Crawley, Jeffrey Cullin, Dominick Curran, Edward Dolan, Jane and Betty Darwin and child, Mary Denny, Mary Donaghan (a child; its mother ?dead ?unknown), Betsy and Eliza Donovan, Arthur, Betsey, Patrick and Catherine Donnelly, John and Edward Doran, William Dwyer, Catherine Dwyer, Mary Ellis, Samuel Fielding, Henry Fisher, John and Michael Fleming, Bridget and Catherine ?Fl..., John Freckleton, Bridget Gaffney, Julia Gallavin, Ann Gibney, Catherine, Daniel, Michael and John Gleeson, William Greenhouse, Patrick Griffin, Sarah Halloran, John

Hannah, Edward Headley, James Harwood, Thomas Healing, Sophia and Mary Ann Hill, James, Mary and Ellinor Hooker, Henry Howard, Samuel, Ellen and Emanuel Hughes, Edward Hughes (lost one child), Edward Jones, Mrs and George Jones, Johanna and John Kelly, Thomas Kelly, Martha and child Kershaw, Daniel Kilmartin,

Michael Kegan, Catherine and Daniel Leary, Thomas James and Mary Ann Leader, William and Margaret Lloyd, Michael Lynch, William Martin, William Mills, James M Maher, Humphrey, Maurice and Joanna Monahan, William Maulin, William Molan, Johanna Molan, Jane and Eliza Murphy, Patrick Murphy, John Murray, James Murtagh, Patrick McAdams, Daniel and Ann McCartney, Elisabeth, James and Jane Ann McClellan, McCombs (on board the pilot Queen of Chester), Daniel McCurran, Mary and John McDonnell, John McFalls, Catherine, Mary and William McGinn, John McLoughlin, Patrick and Ann McManus, James McMaher, James Nangle, Sarah Neesom, Edwin Neesom, Andrew Oulton, William Orange, Louisa Orrell, James O'Brien, Bridget O'Hara, Sarah Pollard, Henry Powell, Michael Quirk, James Radcliffe, Catherine Mary and Patrick Regan, Anne, Thea, James, Catherine and William Reynolds, Edward Rodgers, Joanna Rooney, Michael Rourke, Ellen and Michael Routh, Hannah Roper (two children in the hospital), Daniel Ryder, Mary Sales, William Sanders, Frederick Savage, William Scanlon, Edward Shearon, Emma Shore, Sarah Somerville, Peter Smith, Mary Smith, Sarah Swallow, Elisabeth Swallow, Mary Ann Taylor, Johanna and Honora Tobin, George Tomlinson, Charles Thompson, Elisabeth Thompson, James Walker, Richard Welch, Elisabeth, John and Mary Warburton, Ellen Ward, William Wells, Henry White, Francis and Catherine Woods, Peter Wrigglesworth.

Names of those of the crew saved to date;

Christopher J Austin, Henry Bennet, William Blodgett, first officer J Bragdon, Frederick Braman, Richard Brannon, B Buckley second carpenter, James Cheyn, Henry ?Colver, William P Gibb second officer, Robert Glindinning, William Green, William Gulliver, Thomas Hiller, ?R Jenkiss, John Keeler, Charles D Locke, John McLaughlin, William J Moore, carpenter, Samuel Moody, William M ?Neland, Edward Quimby, William Roberts, Edward

Rogers, James Stockwell, Johnathan Sweet, George Vain, William Wallace, Daniel Wilder and James Wilson.

Passengers rescued by the Queen of the Ocean which didn't leave till 3pm when the rescued passengers on board would have had to watch the burning of the ship and the acute distress of those still on board. The passengers are listed as such: - Crew; Captian Murdoch, William James Moore, carpenter, George Vane, William Blodget, Jonathan Sweet, Richard Brannon, John MCloughlin, Christian Christian, Thomas Hiller, Christopher J Austin, Adam Jones, Charles D Locke, William R Neland, Isaac Stockwell, Charles Nason, John Keeler, W H Pratt, Samuel Moray, Henry Colver and Henry Jones.

The passengers rescued include Whiston H Bristow, London; Patrick McManas, John Horridge, Patrick Oregan, Patrick Mc Mahon, Patrick Griffin, John Kelly, Dennis Cochrane, Peter Smith, Anna Roper Bilston, Birmingham; Mary Maguire, County Cavan; Mary Carey, Thurles. Altogether twenty nine men and only three women.

It seems that half the crew managed to escape on the boats, as they were either very lucky to be in the right place at the right time, perhaps fighting the fire at the rear of the vessel or, perhaps literally, knew the ropes more than the passengers.

A complete list of crew and passengers as published in the London Evening Sun of August 28th 1848 is included here;

Cabin – Mr and Mrs Dow, Mr Southward, Mr Ellis, Mr Thomas Henry, Mr J K Fellowes, Mr Gregg and Mr and Mrs Graham and daughter.

Second Cabin – Mr James Liddall, Mrs Howard and child, Mrs Reynolds, Mrs Roper and two children, Miss M Banning, Mrs Shaw, Mr J H Powell, Mrs Bristow, Mr Murphy and four others.(Whiston Bristow is not mentioned).

Steerage – Mary Ellis, aged 40; John Gleeson, 40 and Michael Gleeson, 35; Maurice Minihan, 22, Michael Fleming, 20; Thomas Haley, 20; Jerry Brisnall, 30; Martin Doherty, 35; Edward Curohy, 30 and Ellen Curohy, 30; Darby Sullivan, 16, and Geoffrey Sullivan, 20; Michael Quick, 39; Nancy Sullivan, 20; Patrick Griffin, 22; Murphy Hanley, 20; Julia Drummy, 48 and James Drummy, 11; Eugene Condon, 27; Patrick Reagan, 23 Mary Reagan, 20, and Catherine Regan,18; William Molan, 42, Ellen Molan,12, Davis Molan, 11 and John Molan, 9; Jane M'Evoy, 25, and Mary M' Evoy, 4; Mary Cashman,39, Mary Cashman 20, Nancy Cashman, 10, and Darby Cashman, 7, Maurice Cashman, 5 and Edmund Cashman, 2; William Brown, 45; Mary Ann Anderson, 24, and Thomas Anderson, 5; Alice Deacon, 27; John Hamon, 24; Patrick M'Manus, 29; Ann Reynolds, 27; James Reynolds, 12, Thomas Reynolds, 10; Catherine Reynolds, 5; and William Reynolds, 3; Mary Smith and infant, 20; Ann M'Manus, 29; Mary Wynn, 24; Mary Ann Gleeson and infant, 24; Philip Gleeson, 3; Patrick Brady, 8; James Murtagh, 18; John Bell, 41 and Emma Bell, 40; James Hely, 41; John Cambs, 20; Ann Smith, 18; Peter Cox, 25,and Richard Cox, 25; Mary Crook, 40; Martha Kershaw, 38, Ann Kershaw, 2, Mary Ann Kershaw 2 and infant; Richard Walsh; Mary Burns; William Freehouse, 20; Henry Fisher, 20; William Scanlan; Samuel Pollinseale, 21; James Sale, 24 and Mary Sale, 24; Sarah Pollard, 20; Henry White, 21; Winfred Keegan, 45; Betsy Mulvoney, 16; Catherine Coyle, 25; Michael Kean, 25; Daniel Kilmartin, 30; Michael Rowk, 25; Thomas Constantine, 47 and Ann Constantine, 47; William Wills, 48 and Mrs Wills, 30; Mary Ann Finan, 3; Jane Roberts, 20; James Walker, 22; John Freckleton, 22; Elisha Bannister, 22; Margaret Flood, 45; Margaret Flood, 15; Catherine Flood, 14; ad Bridget Flood 12; Daniel McCarthy, 26; Sarah Halloran, 14; and Margaret Halloran, 12; Samuel Ryder, 27, and Jane Ryder, 27; George Tomlinson, 25; Peter Wrigglesworth, 26; Rebecca Hill, 36,

Sophia Hill, 9 and Sarah Ann Hill, 9; Georges Jones, 28, and Mrs Jones, 28; Jane Nolan, 22, and Margaret Nolan, 18; William Mavity, 24; Joseph Blyden, 28; Mrs S Neesom, 44, Sarah Neesom, 16, Edward Neesom and Jane Neesom, 17; H Powell,23; Joseph Butterworth, 30; Patrick Murphy, 25; Johanna Kelly, 18; John Brown, 30; Thomas Brown, 8. Frederick Brown, 4, Mrs Brown, 30, and infant; Catherine Clark, 19; Mary Clark, 23, and Isabella Clark, 6; William Sanders, 26; Daniel O'Connor, 30, Mary O'Connor, 28; Charles Thompson, 32, Sarah Thompson, 25, and Alice Thompson, 8, Henry Thompson, 12; James Harwood, 32; Mary Tobin, 38, Honora Tobin, 34, and Johanna Tobin, 26; Johannah Grey, 27; Samuel Hughes, 3 and John Hughes, 14; Dennis Burns, 24, and Eliza Burns, 22; John Murray, 26; James McMahan, 20; Andrew Outlan, 20; Edward Jones and Mary Jones; William Lloyd, 25, and Margaret Lloyd, 22; Eliza Bell,20; Dennis Corcoran, 21; John Dougherty, 40; James Henry, 20; James Connor, 20; Margaret McGee, 20; James Nangle, 55; Dominick Curran, 20; Jas Ronayn, 48, Margaret Ronayn, 48, Margaret Ronayn, 17 Catherine Ronayn, 11, Eliza Ronayn, 9 Johanna Ronayn, 28; Robert Maxwell, 46; John M'Fall, 24; James Booker,61, Mary Booker, 24, and Edwin Booker, 18; Betty Swallow, 30; James Radcliffe, 22; John Johnson, 23; Thomas Brettall, 44, and Jane Brettall, 41; James Winstanley, 27; Lewes Owell, 25; Mary Brittan, 27; John M'loughln, 22; Edward Dolan, 20 and John Dolan, 22; Biddy O'Hara, 18, and Catherine O'Hara, 20; William Scanlan, 60; John Atkinson, 30; Tomas Reynolds, 20; Thomas Lister, 28, Mary Ann Lister, 28 and James Lister, 16; James Durven, Bridget Durven and child; Samuel Fielding, 60; Joseph Shread, 22; William Jackson, 30, Esther Jackson, 30, infant, Elizabeth Jackson, 5 and William Jackson, 3; Thomas Jones, 30 and James Jones, 20; William Bamson, 20; Catherine Dwyn, 25; Arthur Donnelly, 16; William Towns,33; Catherne Grason, 18 and Ann Grason, 29; George Parker, 14; John Kelly, 36; John Warburton,50; Mary Warburton,

18; Edward Hurtley, 20; Norry Galvin, 32 and Julia Galvin, 60; Norry Keating, 30; Catherine Kelly, 18; Norry Callaghan, 18; Dennis Callaghan, 50 and John Callaghan, 14; Mary Dinan, 18; John Moynah, 17; Mary Carey, 13; Darby Donohue, 20; Humphrey Moynahun, 20; Johanna Barry, 25; Edward Kelly, 31, and John Kelly, 34; Catherine Leary, 8 and Dan Leary 11; Thomas Kay, 27, and Mrs Kay, 26; James Wilson, 26; Catharine Wilson, 25, and infant; Edward Sheene, 5 and Margaret Sheene, 50; Peter Smith, 19; Joseph Shaw 28; Mary Shaw, 25; Ann Shaw, 2 and Sarah Shaw, 1; Ann Fielding, 60; Sarah Fisher, 25; Emma Shae, 37; Elizabeth Ward, 24; Sarah Ann Ward, 24, Ann Ward, 9 and Edward Ward, 3; Timothy Coybry, 40; Michael Fanning, 25; Ann Gibney, 20; Catharine Sullivan, 23, Johanna Sullivan, 4 and Ellen Sullivan, 2; Susan Callaghan, 12; James O'Brien, 15; Elizabeth Thompson, 45; Michael Lynch, 21; Margaret Smith, 15, Ellen Smith, 14, Mary Smith, 10, and Thomas Smith, 8; Patrick Delangham, 26; Ellen Ruth, 18, Owen Curley, 21; Frances Spencer, 22; Mary Warburton and infant; Arthur Muldoon, 25; Mary Ann Nessbett, 20; Acles Cuddy, 16; Frances Woods, 18 and Catharine Woods, 17; Margaret Gormly, 17; Ellen Tierney, 55 and Bridget Tierney, 23; Mary A Taylor, 25;Sarah Taylor 4 and G Taylor, 2; Rosanna Green, 25; William Maguire, 27; Ellen Kellerher, 30, and infant; D Gleason, 20 and M Gleason, 15; Nancy Nolan, 17; Ann Murphy, 30; Elizabeth M'Clelland, 32, Jane M'Clelland, 19 and James M'Clelland, 16; Mary M'Guire, 18; Bridget Gafney, 20 and Mary Gafney, 18; M Keegan, 35; Mr W Driston, 30; Mary Maxwell, 20; John George, 33; Margaret Allan; Bridget Regan; Hugh Glynne, 30.

Reading through the passenger lists it is evident that most of those who wanted to emigrate were all of the younger generation with the next generation under their protection and, without needing the assistance of too much imagination if a character is attempted to be put into any of the names, a real human being emerges. And these characters, after the initial excitement or apprehension for the voyage, would have been thrown fully and without preparation into the fear of losing everything including their lives and, those with children, the added dilemma of who to save first in a family of several children. Each at a young adult age had the real fear of burning to death on board the vessel with no evident means of escape, or drowning to death in the cold and unfamiliar sea, adults and children alike. Such is the progress of humanity, as nothing really changes in its conflicts with the natural elements and the eternal conflicts within itself.

~~~~~
~~~~~

SOURCES AND ACKNOWLEDGEMENTS

Newspaper images by kind permission of British Library Newspaper archive via Findmypast The British Newspaper Archive (http/ www.britishnewspaperarchive.co.uk[1]).

Thanks also to David Glover of the Halifax Antiquarian Society for generously taking the time to respond to my enquiry about the possible whereabouts of the remains of the figurehead of the Ocean Monarch, last heard of in Halifax, Yorkshire.

Admiral Grenfell

http://www.grenfellhistory.co.uk/biographies/john_pascoe_grenfell.php

Duke d'Aumale

http://eurochannel.com/en/Henri-d-Orleans-The-Story-behind-the-Duke-of-Aumale.html

J F Froes

https://www.casgliadywerin.cymru/items/617051

Inflation calculator

https://www.in2013dollars.com/uk/inflation/1848?amount=2

In this link there is a representation of the burning of the Ocean Monarch as described in the Forward.

http://www.old-merseytimes.co.uk/OCEANMONARCH.html

The Brazilian rebellion in Pernambuco;

https://translate.google.com/translate?hl=en&sl=pt&u=http://blogs.diariodepernambuco.com.br/historiape/index.php/2016/09/26/joaquim-nunes-machado-um-corajoso-reformista/&prev=search&pto=aue

1. https://www.smashwords.com/profile/view/albarcol81.%20

Metric conversion;-

https://www.google.com/
search?q=acre+conversion+to+hectare&oq=acre+conversion&aqs=chron

John Bramley Moore; Wikipedia

https://en.wikipedia.org/wiki/John_Bramley-Moore

Bloomingdale Hospital

https://en.wikipedia.org/wiki/Bloomingdale_Insane_Asylum

James Young Simpson surgeon

https://www.rcpe.ac.uk/heritage/college-history/
james-young-simpson

Opportunities for migrants;

http://www.thepotteries.org/old_pubs/009.htm

Mourning

https://msu.edu/user/beltranm/mourning/mourning.htm

Elisabeth Helm

https://warwick.ac.uk/fac/arts/history/ecc/archive/emforum/
projects/brieflives/elizabeth_helme/

Marshall Bertrand

https://www.frenchempire.net/biographies/bertrand/

Guy Mannering

https://www.oocities.org/athens/styx/1260/
GuyMannering_History.htm

https://www.newspapers.com/clip/34541429/ship-guy-
mannering-under-quarantine/

Chartists; Most of the story has come from the newspapers but some, especially the results of the trial, and the subsequent fates of the participants in the event is retrieved from here;

http://www.chartistancestors.co.uk/ashton-under-lyne-rising-
1848-a-shot-in-the-dark/

Lancashire Parish Records

https://www.lan-opc.org.uk/

US dollar inflation calculator as used for Jotham Bragdon

https://www.officialdata.org/us/inflation/
1800?amount=1#:~:text=The%20dollar%20had%20an%20average,Labor%
[2]

Other metric conversions

https://www.metric-conversions.org/volume/
uk-gallons-to-liters.htm?val=60

https://www.metric-conversions.org/volume/
uk-quarts-to-liters.htm

https://www.metric-conversions.org/weight/
long-tons-to-metric-tons.htm

https://www.rapidtables.com/convert/weight/
pound-to-kg.html

https://www.officialdata.org/us/inflation/1800?amount=1

More detailed reading about Frederick Jerome here;-

https://vainio.wixsite.com/ourfamilyhistory/stories

Image of the burning of the Ocean Monarch 24th July 1848 https://commons.wikimedia.org/wiki/
File:Ocean_Monarch_1848_byWalters.png

HMS Sceptre; wrecked at Capetown. When a fire broke out down below the smoke became too thick to deal with. This is from both the written account (in private hands) of Johann Sankoffsky, (that old seadog) surviving quarter gunner crew member of the shipwreck and information from the link below;-

https://dawlishchronicles.com/2019/10/11/the-loss-of-hms-sceptre-1799/

2. https://www.officialdata.org/us/inflation/
1800?amount=1%23:~:text=The%20dollar%20had%20an%20average,Labor%20Statistics%
20consumer%20price%20index.

THE OLD SEAFARER AND THE AUTHOR

The hands that typed in the keys to the above account have as one of their origins, the old sea dog, in Johann Sankovsky (Sankoffsky) who was born in 1774 in East Prussia, now Poland, and of German ethnicity. Losing his parents at an early age, he eventually went to sea, and while returning from the East Indies on the Dutch East India company ship the Alblasserdam, his ship was captured off the island of St Helena by the British, and he was taken prisoner. At this point which was during the Napoleonic wars, he opted for service in the British Navy rather than imprisonment as the only other given choice. During some eventful service, he was shipwrecked from the burning British naval man o' war, HMS Sceptre, off Capetown on 5th November 1799 at twenty five years of age, the general, young age of many of the Ocean Monarch passengers. Clinging on to a timber for dear life, he eventually reached the shore.

Having become a part of a multinational crew, he had worked himself up to quarter gunner and left the navy at the end of his service, settling in Carlisle, the home town of a shipmate. Anglicising his surname to Cofty, he eventually worked on the coastal trade from Carlisle to, Liverpool and while one of the sons of his first wife remained in Liverpool, that city of extremes of rich and poor and Catholic and Protestant, the other left for America in 1849. His granddaughter in Liverpool married a seafarer who was one of many who died at sea in an unknown incident and an unknown cause whether it might have been from natural causes, accident, disease, or drowned while escaping from a burning ship is not known. But their only daughter married into a family of bakers who had earlier provided the buns for the fancy fair and would have known acutely the tragedy of the Ocean Monarch.

War and tragedy are never very far away in the human experience and when the 1914 war arrived her children left Liverpool to train in Blackpool as conscripted troops. The son produced through the marriage of one of these troops to his landlady's daughter became a firefighter who during WW2, returned to Liverpool to fight a fire on an American merchant vessel in Liverpool docks when the city itself was burning like the Ocean Monarch. He was knocked unconscious by a snapped and swinging hawser as he manned the high pressure pumps and, dragged off the ship by colleagues, he came-to shortly afterwards to watch the ship explode after its stock of explosives for its hastily constructed, protective guns caught fire.

The viewing of the gravestone of Alice Wrigley at Bispham parish church by the progeny of this generation, initially baptised in the Christian tradition in the church, and whose fingers have tapped the keys to create this account had sent the memories of generations back to Liverpool and the tragedy of the Ocean Monarch where some would have experienced the incident as observers and some, in the bakery trade, might have been called upon to satisfy the demand of the 'fancy fair'. The experience of the tragedies and tribulations of others is never very far away in the interconnections of the generations. We can all shed a tear for Alice, and those that died with her and those that experienced the catastrophe even from this distance in time since human tragedy is still currently represented in every corner of the Earth. Jotham and Frederick and those that were concerned with the wellbeing of others can be saluted for their bravery and selflessness as it is still expressed today in the few that share a concern for others beyond themselves, and is how the human being can continue to survive before it might destroy itself completely, not only in the usually misguided belief in its own individual and collective ascendancy in conflict, but also in declaring ignorance of the conflict with the very earth that the human being inhabits.

~~~~~

Published at Smashwords 2021. Colin Reed Smashwords profile https://www.smashwords.com/profile/view/albarcol81.[1]

1. https://www.smashwords.com/profile/view/albarcol81.%20
~~~~~

Also by Colin Reed

Jimmy Bucklesmith's Unexpected Day Out
The Four Ringtones of the Apocalypse
The Proud Black and White Speckled Hen
Masterpiece
Identikit
Last Orders at Waterloo
The Man O' The Woods
Skipdoll
Yer Main Ingerland Man
The Queue for the Bog
Coming Clean
The Lion and the Cheesegrater
L for Louisa
In Heaven's Glorious Bosom
Myra Thorndyke's Very Last Affair
Collection Short Stories 1
The Last Words of a Good Man
The Skinless Guest
A Bad Day for an Urban Sasquatch
Mrs Gigglebottom Is Always Busy
Blackpool and the Fylde During WW1
Mr Gigglebotom Goes To Work
The Tragedy of the Ocean Monarch
Cissie Loftus. Versatile Music Hall Entertainer and Actress

The Conception, Construction and Opening of the Tower at Blackpool 1890-1894

Watch for more at cmronline.co.uk.

www.ingramcontent.com/pod-product-compliance
Lightning Source LLC
LaVergne TN
LVHW020010170826
845677LV00022B/2052